Pioneers in Ministry

Women Pastors in Ontario
Mennonite Churches, 1973-2003

Pioneers in Ministry

Women Pastors in Ontario Mennonite Churches, 1973-2003

By Mary A. Schiedel

Published by Pandora Press
Co-published with Herald Press
2003

National Library of Canada Cataloguing in Publication

Schiedel, Mary
    Pioneers in ministry : Women Pastors in Ontario Mennonite Churches, 1973-
2003 / Mary Schiedel.

Co-published with Herald Press.
ISBN 1-894710-35-5

    1. Mennonite Church Eastern Canada—Biography.
2. Mennonites—Clergy—Canada—Biography. 3. Women
clergy—Canada—Biography. 4. Mennonite women—Canada—Biography. I. Title.

BX8141.S34 2003   289.7'092   C2003-902111-4

Pioneers in Ministry:Women Pastors in Ontario Mennonite Churches, 1973-2003
    Copyright©2003 by Pandora Press
    33 Kent Avenue
    Kitchener, Ontario N2G 3R2
    www.pandorapress.com
    All rights reserved
    Co-published with Herald Press
    Scottdale, Pennsylvania/Waterloo, Ontario

    International Standard Book Number: 1-894710-35-5
    Book design by Julia Stark
    Cover design by Christian Snyder
    Cover Art: Graphite drawing "Of Her Was Born" by Susan D. Shantz
    1981, 11" X 12"

13 12 11 10 09 08 07 06 05 04 03   12 11 10 9 8 7 6 5 4 3 2 1

To
all of our co-workers in the churches, conference offices, and
pulpits of the Mennonite churches in Ontario

Table Of Contents

Acknowledgments

I want to thank many people for their encouragement of my writing of this book. First of all I appreciate the time, and effort of the twenty-four women pastors who wrote responses to my original questions and shared their stories and photos. I recognize the courage it took to do so, and the vulnerable position these women are in when making their stories public.

I also appreciate the encouragement and help of Muriel Bechtel, the Minister of Pastoral Services, and the assistance of Catherine Hunsberger and Lorraine Sawatsky in helping to compile and collect information for our lists of women pastors.

My neighbour, Joanne Mead Nadeau, put energy and enthusiasm into photography. I thank her for the work on my personal photos . I am grateful that my niece, Susan Shantz, has given us permission to reproduce her drawing for the cover. I would also like to thank Christian Snyder, of Pandora Press, for designing the cover.

I thank Pandora Press for their work on this project. I have appreciated the expertise, guidance and interest of Julia Stark, my editor. I also appreciate the sponsorship of the book by the Institute of Anabaptist Mennonite Studies, Conrad Grebel University College.

I want to acknowledge and thank the people in the churches I have been involved with for their encouragement and support of my work as a pastor. Without many of you this story would not have been told.

Other women pastors who felt they did not have the time or energy to respond at this time also affirmed this writing project and gave their support and encouragement as well. My advisory group, Doris, Hendrike and Sue, met faithfully throughout the past year. They helped to shape this writing project and gave valuable counsel along the way.

Preface

The women pastors in Mennonite Church Eastern Canada are ordinary women who, "by the power of God at work within them," have done extraordinary things. In telling their stories, Mary Schiedel reminds us that these too have been among the earthen vessels who bore a precious treasure and made a difference in Mennonite Church Eastern Canada. These women have been witnesses to the power of God in their lives, and agents of God's love and mercy to those whom they have been called to serve. They persisted, some against great odds, to claim their calling. They wore the mantle of leadership with grace and courage when others around them were not yet able to affirm them in their decisions to pursue and prepare for a career in pastoral ministry.

These stories need to be told, not because they are more important than others, but because they help us to remember and honour the contributions of women who sought to be faithful to God's call. Many of these women ministered in congregations where no woman had previously served as a pastor. They show us what we have learned, and point us toward steps we have yet to take. Perhaps in reading these contemporary "sacred texts," more women, and also men, will be prodded to consider whether God is calling them to pastoral ministry.

As she tells these stories, Mary also shares about those times and places where their lives have intersected with hers, illustrating the way women have grown and thrived in ministry—by drawing strength and wisdom from each other. For in both church and world, women still contend with practices and theological understandings that do not welcome them into leadership roles. Furthermore, when we do have the privilege of working together as women and men, all too often we get into power struggles, comparisons and miscommunications that are harmful to ourselves and our ministries. We desperately need women and men who recognize their need for everyone's gifts, who welcome each other's leadership, and who are committed to working together in mutually supportive ways. Hopefully these women's experiences will inspire coming generations of leaders, both women and men, to continue working at creating effective and mutually satisfying ways of being colleagues and partners in ministry.

By honouring the past and illuminating the present, Mary shines a light down the path toward a promising future. Just as later generations of women pastors benefitted from the courage and faithfulness of those who have pioneered the way, so the future will be shaped by a new generation of creative and imaginative women and men who are heirs to the legacy in this book. May the seeds that were sown by these women continue to grow and bear fruit for generations to come.

Muriel Bechtel, Minister of Pastoral Services, Mennonite Church Eastern Canada
November, 2002
Kitchener, Ontario

Introduction: The Work of Our Hands and Our Hearts

People have asked me, regarding this project, whether I was asked to write about women pastors. I was encouraged to write by a few women pastors In the Mennonite Church Eastern Canada who suggested that somebody should write our stories—especially those from the early days. When I got more serious about doing it, and I checked to see how many women have been serving the church in Ontario in pastoral ministry, I found that the number was too large to record each one's complete story.

Even by limiting my project to those women pastors who have served in a congregation in Ontario for at least two years, I had a list numbering high in the forties! In addition, there are a few dozen more women who have worked in youth ministry or chaplaincy. I knew that I could not include everyone—and certainly not everyone's story! I leave the writing of their complete stories to the women themselves as they find time and opportunity to do so. Of course, I have had to work with the women who chose to respond and to write part of their stories. There have been twenty-four who have responded at some length; several are quoted more briefly.

Other good questions that have come up are "Who are you writing for?" and "Who will be your readers?" I hope some readers will have known these women, or will have lived through these years of change in

13

the Mennonite Church Eastern Canada, and in the broader Mennonite Church. I also hope this book will be available in many church libraries. If you have been part of a church with a woman pastor, I hope you read about that experience, and about other women pastors and churches throughout the Mennonite Church. I also welcome readers from other backgrounds and faith traditions.

As to "Who are you writing for?" Primarily I am writing for the Mennonite Church which I chose to join, and of which I have been a part for many years. It is the church where I was nurtured in faith, and where I have been called to serve in various ways during my lifetime— including thirteen years in pastoral ministry in three different congregations. I want to affirm those churches for taking the risk of calling a woman as pastor. It does require an openness to God's leading in a new direction, and is a definite step of faith. Of course I am also writing for the women who have shared some of their stories, and who have made this book possible.

I appreciate the support given to me by my reference group for this project: Hendrike Isert-Bender, Sue Steiner and Doris Weber who met with me faithfully, and provided good counsel and much encouragement. As we read and reflected on the material which came in, some interesting themes emerged from the responses from women pastors. I chose to work with several of these themes. It surprised me that I knew almost all of the women who responded, and so I decided to weave my own reflections around their responses. In this way I am sharing my own story, and am partly writing for myself!

Am I a feminist? Possibly, and if so, definitely a Christian feminist. I have always been a free thinker. I suspect that has as much to do with my love of reading, and with being the second youngest in a family of eight, as with my being a woman. My nurturing in the Christian faith came from church and family, but I can also identify the ongoing influence of writers of devotional books and columns. Often they were women, and I felt a kinship with their down-to-earth spirituality and theology. I tend to consider traditional theology to be basically male, but I have always wanted "To light a candle rather than curse the darkness."

When I returned from a teaching assignment in Kenya with Mennonite Central Committee in the Teachers' Abroad Programme, I was ready to consider more education or job options. In the mid-seventies I attended a "Women in Ministry" conference in Kitchener sponsored by the MCC Task Force on Women, Church and Society. That was an exciting experience for those of us who participated, and I enjoyed other such conferences over the years. I have also appreciated the "Women Doing Theology" conference which began in Waterloo in 1992, sponsored by the Canadian Committee on Women's Concerns. These conferences have continued to involve and challenge women pastors and others throughout Canada and the United States.

After my call to ministry, I began seminary studies part-time at Waterloo Lutheran Seminary. One study I did in a basic New Testament course at WLS clearly related to a Biblical basis for my ministry. I am grateful to Kristen Stendahl for his work, and I claim Galatians 3:28 as a text for my ministry: "Faith in Christ Jesus is what makes each of you equal with the other, whether you are a Jew or a Greek, a slave or a free person, a man or a woman." A deeper and long-standing affirmation for me comes from the way Jesus accepted women he met, and also accepted the ministry of one woman who anointed him for burial.

Personally I recognize two women from outside the Mennonite church who influenced me. Dr. Mary Malone, a retired Professor of theology formerly at St. Jeromes, University of Waterloo, inspired me with her lectures and her writing. In her most recent book, *Women and Christianity* Vol. II, she writes about Beguine spirituality in the thirteenth century in a way that relates to the stories of women in this book: "It is surely one of the greatest gifts of this women's movement that they found themselves able to prove from their own experience that they were created in the image of God." In the '70's and '80's women pastors were not usually "called" in the same way that their male colleagues had been. I believe that for women the call related to personal growth in their own sense of worth and was often grounded in the awareness of being created in God's image.

The other woman who influenced me more recently as I continued in ministry was Rev. Dr. Muriel Carder, a retired Baptist missionary to India, and earlier a lecturer in New Testament Greek at McMaster University. Later she was a professor at Andhra Christian Theological College (Inter-denominational) in Hyderabad, India. Muriel was my supervisor in a clinical pastoral education experience in 1989, and she both challenged and encouraged me in the Woodstock community-based unit before I accepted more responsibility at Elmira the following year. Muriel has also been a spiritual director to me during the past fifteen years.   At the age of eighty, she is still active in ministry as a retired chaplain in Woodstock, Ontario, and as an elder in the First Baptist Church.

Twenty-four women have contributed to this book. They have responded to some probing questions I asked them about their disappointments and joys in ministry, and about how they were sustained in their calling as pastors. Some interesting and helpful things have emerged in relation to ministering alone, to team ministry and to family and pastoring. These themes appear in several sections. My own hope in writing is to set out some of the experiences, reflections and stories of these female leaders, who have worked for at least two years as pastors ministering in the Mennonite churches of Ontario through the work of their hands and their hearts.

I hope you enjoy reading this book, and find time to reflect on our comments and experiences. The responses have all come from women in Ontario where most of the churches in Mennonite Church Eastern Canada are located. The story of women pastors in MCEC is not finished. All of us still have some things to learn and a significant part to play in releasing the gifts of women in this form of ministry. I trust that you will note the variety of gifts which we have, as well as our unique experiences and personalities. I believe that God has had some significant work for us to do. I trust that God will bless and establish the work of our hands and of our hearts.

April, 2003

Women Pastors In Ontario Writing Project

These questions were sent, in January 2002, to about fifty women pastors in Mennonite churches in Ontario. Twenty-four women responded to the questions, or shared their stories in some other way. I interviewed only five of the women. I also invited further responses from others in order to provide a balanced picture.

Here are some questions for your reflection. Choose those that you can best relate to, and please respond, if at all possible, to at least one in each section. I trust that it will be useful for you to do this exercise.

What is your image of ministry, and how have you worked with it?

What have been the greatest joys, disappointments or struggles for you?

What has surprised you most in pastoral ministry?

What important experiences in ministry have confirmed your sense of call?

What has empowered you—kept you going?

What is your most significant contribution in ministry?

Where is your call leading you in ministry at this time?

What is your vision for women pastors in the Mennonite Church?

In your response, tell a part of your story that connects with a question, or give an anecdote from your experience in pastoral care or which you have used in a sermon.

TRAILBLAZERS

"These women were trailblazers, each in her own unique way."
—Mary Schiedel

In the Mennonite churches of Ontario, women pastors have been serving since the early 1970s. Of course, women had served in many significant ways long before that. Women will continue to be an important part of the church in the future in many other roles—perhaps some as new and different as the role of the female pastor has been. The actual number of women who have been, or presently are, pastors in Ontario Mennonite churches is about fifty in 2003. Most of these women have also been ordained or licensed. A pastor in the Mennonite Church is licensed at the beginning of a pastoral assignment. Usually after two years, and at the recommendation of the church involved, the pastor will be ordained with Conference officials participating in the ordination service. Commissioning provided credentials for ministry in a specific church or ministry setting and was used, primarily in the 1970s.

The Mennonite Church has origins in the Anabaptist movement in Europe in the sixteenth century. The church is named after Menno Simons, a former Roman Catholic priest in the Netherlands, who was one of the early leaders of the group which was persecuted by church and state officials for their illegal practice of re-baptizing persons as adults. Small groups of Anabaptists met secretly for Bible study, and women were active in leadership along with men. In the *Martyrs Mirror* there are stories of Anabaptist women and men who died for their beliefs. In 2003 the Mennonite Church, which is relatively small, has a worldwide membership with over half of the members living in the southern hemisphere. While there are Mennonite churches spread across Canada, major concentrations of Mennonites are in Manitoba and Ontario.

The Mennonite Church has recently undergone a major change as three branches of Anabaptist Mennonites have come together. The Ontario Mennonite Conference, which became the Mennonite Conference of Ontario and Quebec, and the Western Ontario (Amish) Mennonite Conference shared a Conference Minister in the 1970s. Then the United Mennonite churches of Ontario, with origins in the Russian Mennonite immigration to Canada, also began working together with the first two groups in a joint Inter-Mennonite Conference. In 1987 the three groups were "integrated" into the Mennonite Conference of Eastern Canada. The most recent name change occurred in the year 2001 when the Conference became the Mennonite Church Eastern Canada following the formation several years earlier of Mennonite Church Canada as a church distinct from the Mennonite Church U.S.A.

The advent of women pastors in the offices and pulpits of Ontario Mennonite churches has been another change during the last thirty years, and one which has occurred in several phases. From 1976 to 1978, Alma Coffman was a pastor at the Ottawa Mennonite Church. In each branch of the church at least one woman had been ordained by 1982: Martha Smith was commissioned in 1977; Doris Weber was commissioned/ ordained in 1979; Doreen Neufeld was ordained in 1980; Martha Smith

Good was ordained in 1982; and Bertha Landers was the sole pastor at Bloomingdale Mennonite by 1982. These women pastors were trailblazers, each in her own unique way. Because it was a new experience for the church to have a woman as a minister, there was some confusion at times in the conferences and congregations, and also some pain—especially for the women involved. I'm grateful to them for the vision and fortitude they had as they pioneered in an often difficult environment.

The five women who are the first group of Mennonite women pastors in Ontario deserve special recognition for being pioneers who suffered through some of the difficult adjustments and changes that had to be made by their colleagues in the churches and in the seminaries where they trained. As the first women to pastor in their congregations, they also deserve credit for ministering so effectively that other churches became more open to calling women as pastors.

Doris Weber

"Life is simply too short to wear masks and play games."
—D. W.

Doris Weber began ministry with her husband, Rod, at the Avon Mennonite Church in the early '70s. She and Rod were both commissioned by the Western Ontario Mennonite Conference in 1979. Since then, commissioning has been accepted as a form of ordination. In recent years, Doris has served as an Interim Pastor at quite a few churches: Valleyview (London), Waterloo North, Danforth (Toronto), Mannheim, and Bloomingdale. She has been a pastor for more than twenty years.

I learned to know Doris at Associated Mennonite Biblical Seminaries in Elkhart, Indiana, where we both were studying in 1984-85. Later we were together in a small mutual support group for women pastors for some years. I appreciate Doris's down-to-earth approach to ministry, her sense of humour and her encouragement and goodwill toward other women pastors. She is a mother to six adult children and a grandmother to sixteen. Doris and Rod are now retired; they live on Doris's home farm on Sandhills Road in Wilmot Township. Doris has reflected on her ministry and she shares from her varied experiences in her usual candid and engaging way.

Growing up as a child in WOMC, my parents took us to many musical events held in other churches. Denomination did not matter. On one such occasion, when I was between nine and eleven years old, the female pastor of the church introduced the musicians. The next morning I asked my mother if she thought I might be able to be a pastor some day. She was true to her teaching and replied that she did not think so. However, the spark continued to burn within me. I read avidly. I remember buying a small book on the Virgin Birth for twenty-five cents. I would read and study it in the evening before going to bed, sitting over the heating register in the upstairs hall.

The call to ministry was something within me that longed for expression. I attended OMBS (Ontario Mennonite Bible School) and OMBI (Ontario Mennonite Bible Institute) in Kitchener. My gifts were affirmed, even though the pastorate was not overtly mentioned. This call was so strong that when I was contemplating marriage in my mid-twenties, I told my husband-to-be that I wanted to work in the church after our marriage. He was agreeable, although neither of us knew at the time how this would work itself out.

After marriage, our children were born in rapid succession. Six in nine years. There was no time to actively pursue the call, but it did not die. It was as if I put it on a shelf and would from time to time take it off the shelf, dust it, hold it to my heart, put it back and return to my family duties. So it was that when my youngest child entered school I too went back to school. I received my BA and my M.Div. It was while I was studying that I began co-pastoring with my husband. The call I had felt so early and intensely was coming to fruition. I had come home to a part of myself that was separate from my family and was finally being fulfilled.

I have several images of ministry and all are closely related. In many ways they are unconscious, and yet they are the basis on which my ministry has been built. Isaiah 49:16 declares that the Lord has inscribed Israel in the palm of his hands. My belief is that this is equally true for me as a follower of Christ. It is a safe, secure and loved place in which to rest. KJV translates this verse as saying that God holds us in the palm of His hand. Since my early years this has been a great comfort for me.

Above all else God is love. In my mind's eye, I see God with outstretched arms calling and inviting me. Consequently my ministry is one of love. I must experience and know love as a certainty, and then I can invite others to reach out, receive, live, and be challenged by the one who is Love. God's love enables me to love people as they are, and yet challenge them as to what they might be. Do not be mistaken; this is not a lethargic, cushy love. It is a constant challenge to growth and new life in Christ. Always, who I am is as important as what I say.

Another image I have is that there is a song that sings deep within me. My hope is that all of us together will sing God's Song. Yet another image is that there is a party going on as in the story of the Prodigal Son. My work of ministry is to clarify the invitation to God's party, and to invite any and all to the party.

The opportunity that ministry gave to me to share my life and heart with others, even as they shared theirs with me, has been a great joy. I listened to others so that they could speak their truth and act upon it. It is gratifying to know that I do not need to have all the answers: it was in listening that people found their answers. It remans a joy and wonder that God can use me in spite of my inadequacies and mixed feelings.

The times that my ideals and words and actions were very far apart were always disappointing to me. I have been disappointed at the blindness of Anabaptist Mennonites to their intolerances, and the refusal to look honestly at them. At times, it would seem to me, that once we are Christians and in the Church, we have no need for repentance. There are respectable needs and failures which we as a people confess, and yet some of the deepest pains of our lives are not acceptable.

I have been disappointed that some people found my gender a block to both affirming and confronting me. One Sunday morning I preached a sermon on Ezekiel's dry bones, and invited the listeners to allow God's breath of the life-giving Spirit to blow and bring life to the dry bones that might be part of their lives. In this particular congregation one of the disgruntled male members, who could hardly look at me, much less shake hands with me, phoned on Monday morning asking to speak to Rod. He asked Rod to tell me that my sermon had touched him deeply, and that there was the warm glow of new life and love in his heart.

As a mother and wife, one of my ongoing struggles was juggling home, family, and ministry. It was a struggle not to feel guilty about what I could not do due to lack of time and energy. There were times that I knew I could have done better and possibly been more effective if there were not so many divided interests.

Another struggle arose out of co-pastoring. Even though our approach to ministry was miles apart, I was grateful for the support of my husband. The difference in our pastoring styles was partly due to gender differences, but also because of the people we were and the environments we had grown up in. My husband was born on the prairie and I was born in Southern Ontario, resulting in varied ways of thinking. We were both ordained on March 8, 1979 at Avon Mennonite Church in Stratford. The struggle was one of being true to myself and what I believed. Later on, when Rod and I began to work in separate churches, it eliminated that area of struggle. Co-pastoring has its challenges. For example, the congregation will often compare between the two pastors which can add challenges to a marriage. Also, it is easy to let planning time take over family time. Division of labour was also difficult because we were both good at pastoral visiting, so we had to decide who was going to visit who. Often people would say they had had no visit if Rod had not been there. However, co-pastoring has many benefits, such as bringing different viewpoints to the issue at hand, work sharing, and mutual support.

I was very surprised at how much I liked preparing sermons. The entire process, from the beginning research for a sermon to the writing and delivery of it, was a very rewarding and gratifying experience. Sermon preparation and delivery are a very personal and moving experience for me. One Sunday morning after the worship service a young woman, seventeen to eighteen years old, sought me out. She said that she wanted me to know that even though she had been attending church all of her life she had never bothered to listen to the sermon. However, since I had been preaching, she listened. Her words were affirming of my endeavours to make my sermons relevant to everyone. If I made the sermons understandable to teenagers and children, then certainly the adults would understand too. I didn't use my education and experience to speak above the young people's heads. They were part of the congregation so they had to be included.

However, I was surprised to know how few people really listened to what I had prayerfully struggled to prepare. If they did hear and comment, it would be on what I had thought was quite a minor point. It remains a constant surprise how God's Spirit uses the same words to reach people in many different ways. My sense of call has been confirmed by how people have listened when I preached. Sometimes I have felt shivers go up my back when I see the expectant and listening faces. I have been affirmed many times for my preaching.

I also receive affirmation for my pastoral care. I believe that at most times, I have a non-threatening presence. I see it as a gift that God has given to me; and yet there are times when I am uncomfortable with my borderline introverted nature. In one interim situation, I heard that a certain man in the congregation had some difficulties with me as a woman pastor. I decided to visit him, and in the course of the conversation, he assured me he had no problem with me as a person. In fact, if he were sick, he would be glad to have me visit him. However, he said, that if he should die, he would want someone else to conduct his funeral. I told him that I would respect his wishes in such a situation. Fortunately, he is still living!

As a female minister it was not long until I encountered the "glass ceiling," the ceiling that is known only by the ones who encounter it. There were no written rules, just some vaguely spoken ones, but I knew clearly when I had committed a "no no." Fortunately, as time passed the ceiling began to move and evaporate.

Pot luck dinners were a tricky issue in my time. Were women pastors expected to bring a dish to the pot luck? Or, since we were ministers, was there no need to because we had been serving spiritual food?

Gender differences in preaching are hard to define, and generalizations are often inaccurate. It may be true that at times women are more nurturing in their preaching and ministry. Because of the multi-tasking that was required of me as wife, mother, and home-maker, my illustrations were certainly more earthly and related to daily life.

I remember well when an influential male minister said to me that I was a concrete thinker. I immediately thought of Kohlberg and his stages of development which stated that to move throught the conrete to the abstract thinking was the highest order. Maybe so, but I continue to preach using concrete illustrations and metaphors. For me, life is not lived in abstract thought, as it might be by my male counterparts. It is in the concrete reality that I meet God.

Being female influenced my teaching and preaching with the awareness of women's issues and the passion I had for them. I heard the stories of women and could not ignore them. Because of them, inclusive language was important. Addressing God with a variety of names, rather than using "Father" in most prayers, became an important issue for me. Certainly not all women in the church had loving fathers, and exclusively naming God as father raised hurdles too large to cross. A positive result was that as my naming vocabulary increased so did my concept of God. I soon realized that all words are inadequate to describe God.

I remember well the Sunday I preached on the woman with the hemorrhage in Luke 8. I contemporized it by speaking about women who have been abused in their own homes. Surely the isolation and shame they feel is no less than the woman in the Biblical story, and to reach out and be healed has taken great courage and the risk of misunderstanding. However, healed they can be, and Jesus' reponse to them is the same as to the woman in the story: "Your faith has made you whole." Jesus, the Christ, gives these women personal credit for their work and effort in their own healing. That particular Sunday I was detained at the church until mid-afternoon. Woman after woman came to tell me her story. I was reminded once again that the stories of the lives of the women in the pew were important and needed to be addressed. I left grateful that I had taken the risk to name the unmentionable, and knew deep within me that God loves each of us equally and longs for each person's healing and freedom.

The most basic staying empowerment is my deep sense of call that has not been shaken. When I was working as a chaplain at St. Mary's Hospital, I learned many worthwhile lessons. The greatest was that when illness and disaster deeply tested my faith, many of my theological theories became irrelevant. The one abiding and sustaining belief that grew ever stronger was that God loves me. I have often said that in seminary I learned how to talk; and at the hospital I learned how to keep quiet and listen.

My highest learning curve for ministry took place at St. Mary's. Despite how growth-producing and life-enhancing my work was at the hospital, there was this gut feeling that I was not where I belonged. When I work in congregational ministry, I have this deep gut feeling, a knowing, that I am where I am supposed to be. My sense of call is one of God's great gifts of grace in my life.

I believe that my most significant contribution in ministry is my listening and loving. On that basis I deal with reality as it is, openly and honestly. Life is simply too short to wear masks and play games.

Martha Smith Good

"As I read through the Gospels, I discovered a model which was far superior to any I had read about in contemporary books. I noted specifically how Jesus ministered to people he met, and those who came seeking him."
—M. S. G.

Martha Smith Good was the first woman ordained to pastoral ministry in the Mennonite Conference of Ontario and Quebec. She was the first woman pastor I knew. Soon after Martha came to Kitchener, I heard her speak at a Rockway Mennonite School Women's Association annual meeting, and after that I heard her speak or met her in various settings. I attended her ordination at the Guelph Mennonite Church where she was the pastor for six years. When I began in ministry at Elmira, I was pleased to have her as my mentor during the first year or so. She was an encouraging and insightful person, and I looked forward to my meetings with her. Although Martha has ministered in other settings, including eight years as campus pastor at Goshen College, I am happy that she returned to Ontario in 2000, and is pastor of the Warden Woods Mennonite Church in Scarborough. Martha reflects on her experience in ministry:

When I entered the pastoral ministry there were no women I could look to and say, "Now there is someone I would like to pattern my ministry after." I stood at the bedside of a gravely ill young woman and found I had no words of comfort or reassurance to offer. My task, after all, was to do her morning care, change her bed linen, and make her as physically comfortable as possible. It was not my responsibility to be a social worker or a chaplain. I was a nurse. I felt I had not done enough, and yet what else could I do? I pondered the awareness of feeling inadequate at times of crisis in the life of patients, and the passion that I had to offer more than a bed bath and clean linen.

Entering Goshen College in the fall of 1968 was the beginning of a journey which felt promising, yet unknown. Why was I there? I thirsted for knowledge. I wanted to study, to discover who I was, and to find greater fulfillment for my life. Since I had many years of nursing experience and felt comfortable and secure in a hospital setting, I chose chaplaincy training during my years in seminary as the direction to take to realize my ongoing passion of broadening my healthcare ministry. Furthermore, I believed the church would more quickly accept a woman hospital chaplain than a woman into congregational pastoral ministry.

I began exploring congregational ministry in the summer of 1973 as a pastoral intern in an Ohio congregation. I received much affirmation from lay members in this congregation and encouragement to continue in ministry. After a year as a hospital chaplain in La Junta Colorado, I returned a year later as an assistant to the pastor.

Several challenges loomed large and seemed to threaten my desire, and my call, to pastoral ministry. Since there were so few women in ministry in the early 1970s, I longed for a role model and found none. Books which were written on developing gifts and abilities for the pastoral minister were based on the assumption that pastors were male. I could not identify with the assumptions and wondered how I would find my way. Not knowing where else to look, I began to search the scriptures, particularly the Gospels.

As I read through the Gospels, I discovered a model which was far superior to any I had read about in contemporary books. I noted specifically how Jesus ministered to people he met, and those who came seeking him. He was always compassionate, caring, forgiving and kind, except toward the religious leaders. He was very responsive to those oppressed by social and religious structure. I knew he understood my struggles. I began to ask questions like: "Who was Jesus?," "How did he know what his role was?," "Who was his mentor?," and "Where was his source of strength?" The answer to these questions was in Luke 4:18-19: "The Spirit of the Lord is upon me, because he has anointed me to bring good news to the poor. He has sent me to proclaim release to the captives and recovery of sight to the blind, to let the oppressed go free, to proclaim the year of the Lord's favour." I chose these words for my own basis for ministry, knowing that to follow this model one could not go too far off course. I continue to hold these verses before me as my model, and a goal to move towards.

A second challenge was claiming my position as equal to my pastoral colleagues, all of whom were male at that time. I found myself face to face with a structure, dominated by men, that was reluctant to share assumed power with a female in pastoral partnership. I was still expected to serve snacks to an all-male board of elders, even though one of them had provided the snacks. When asked to do so, I gently declined, noting that I thought the one who provided could also do the serving. In refusing I had begun to set boundaries for myself, a necessary choice if I was to survive and develop my own unique pastoral style.

The most difficult and painful challenge was the denial of my request for ordination by the Mennonite Conference of Ontario and Quebec. Following several meetings, and many painful conversations with conference leadership, I was ordained in April, 1982. I still remain baffled about the initial hesitation as no clear reasons were ever articulated to me. While breaking the sound barrier and gaining recognition as a pastoral minister was extremely hard work, the rewards have far outweighed the difficulties. I found what was missing at the bedside of the gravely ill woman. I learned how to offer words of comfort, to console, pray for, and listen to the needs of others.

I learned how to give of myself, and be myself, and let that be a gift to the one in need, recognizing the gift was not coming from me, but from God through me. It is an awesome responsibility, but a very sacred trust. Some of the highlights are celebrating the birth of a new baby, officiating at a marriage ceremony, baptizing a young Christian, watching a person grow in maturity of faith—to mention only a few. The journey with individuals between the beginning and end of life continues to be exciting for me.

There is also the aspect of walking with someone and his or her family at the end of life's journey toward death. It is then especially when there is an acute realization of the human inability to control life's process. Whether witnessing a birth, which was part of my nursing career, or accompanying someone through to his or her final breath, both are part of life's most sacred experiences. Both are filled with an unexplainable divine presence, and can take individuals home to eternal life.

Would I make this journey again if given an opportunity to relive my life? Definitely! How was I able to make this journey and remain encouraged and enthusiastic about pastoral ministry? I felt the call and blessing of God. I received the support of other women on similar journeys. Their wisdom, our corporate laughter, and common tears have all been most significant as I tried to maintain a healthy perspective on my journey. Will I continue in ministry? I will be responsible in completing my current assignment and then hope to move into retirement. After almost thirty years of ministry, I am aware of generalized fatigue which is possibly the result of many years of work in a sometimes unfriendly environment. This feeling of fatigue resonates with women of my era who made the same journey. Perhaps it is time for us to remove the cloak of office, claim and embrace the work we have done with joy, and offer our skills and insights to the younger women who are beginning the journey. Truly, I believe that while we have come a long way, the journey for greater recognition of women in leadership is ongoing, and perhaps still not easy for some. May God help each of us to "Proclaim the year of the Lord's favour."

Doreen Neufeld

"I have been surprised at the richness of God's blessing. And, yes, the first surprise was that God could really have called me into ministry."
—D. N.

Doreen Neufeld was the first woman ordained in the United Mennonite Church in Ontario. I met Doreen when she was working as a co-pastor at the Welcome Inn in Hamilton. Later she and her husband, Hugo, were Missions Ministers for the Mennonite Church of Eastern Canada. Doreen led mission workshops, spoke in churches, and planned church-wide Mission Festivals during those years. At present she is a co-pastor with Hugo at the Trinity Mennonite Church in Calgary, Alberta. As she approaches retirement, Doreen reflects on her ministry:

In my growing up years, pastoral ministry was something that was clearly reserved for men – mostly somber, older men, with some notable exceptions. I did not dream of becoming a pastor because it was unthinkable for a woman. I was convinced that there were both sociological and theological barriers. Besides, it was too high a calling for me. However, it was very clear that I was called to some form of "ministry" in the Christian church. At sixteen I began teaching Sunday School and Vacation Bible School, and continued delighting in these ministries for the next fifteen years, until our own children kept me too busy. For some years I expected a clear call of some kind to the mission field, which was acceptable for women. But the call never came. When we moved to the Welcome Inn in Hamilton, I became more involved in ministry with adults, especially women, without realizing that perhaps this was the call to the mission field.

Many years before the more direct call to pastoral ministry was named, I had reason to work through the theological issues when a woman in our church was being challenged for using her gifts to lead the mixed adult choir in the church we were attending. To my astonishment, my study of the Scriptures gave me much more freedom to work in the church than I had ever imagined possible. Thus, ten years later I was eventually able to say "yes" when ordination was suggested to me.

I now see pastoral ministry more as shepherding or guiding people much like myself who may not have had the calling or the opportunities for study that I have had. Although it is a very serious calling, it is not necessarily a somber vocation, but an opportunity to laugh and cry with people and remind them of God's abiding presence in every situation in life. It is also to remind people that though God's expectations of us are high, they are there for our benefit.

The greatest joy in my ministry has been to see change in people. It is a pleasure and an honour to be one of God's instruments in bringing healing and wholeness to a human being. It has been a wonderful thing to have the wider Mennonite Church community affirm me in my calling. A disappointment is that in spite of the fact that women have ministered effectively in our Mennonite churches for more than twenty years, there are still many churches and individuals who cannot accept this as possibly being God's will. A church in another denomination which I recently attended has ten pastors, only one of them a woman, who heads up the women's ministries of that congregation. There are still many in the Christian church, including members of my own extended family, who are not convinced that a woman is an acceptable minister in God's eyes.

My struggles with my own self-image become greater when I see others reject me offhand on the basis of my gender. A number of years ago I was asked to conduct a funeral in a Funeral Home. My husband came with me when we went to make arrangements with the Funeral Home Director. The man was simply unable to talk to me, addressing all his comments and questions to my husband, even though I had initiated the conversation and told him I was doing the funeral. It wasn't until my husband turned away and refused to answer that the Director turned to me to complete plans for the funeral.

Truthfully, I was surprised at the courage of the Conference Minister at the time of my ordination for ordaining a woman when it had not been done before in our conference—and there were surely people who would be opposed. Secondly, I was surprised that there was no overt opposition. I have also been surprised at how well I have generally been received, in spite of exceptions. I have been surprised at the richness of God's blessing. And, yes, the first surprise was that God could really have called me into ministry.

I shall never forget the joy and excitement of my first ministry setting, the Welcome Inn. I knew I had an important message for the people in the inner city, and they were eager to hear it. I soon realized that there was nothing I had done before in all my life (I was in my forties by then) --with the exception of parenting—that could compare with the joy and "rightness" of the preaching ministry. I had been doing most of the other pastoral tasks in the same setting for a number of years, without realizing they were pastoral ministry. There is generally a phase during which I struggle with a sermon. I pray a lot, and realize that this is more than a speech. I cannot do it in my own strength. During the presentation and afterwards I am particularly aware of God's presence and affirmation.

The affirmation of God's Spirit within me has been the greatest driving force. Second has been my husband's encouragement. He encouraged me first of all to accept ordination, and we were ordained at the same time. Because I was in the "unique" category, many opportunities opened up for me – to preach in various congregations, to work on conference-wide committees, and to write articles or be interviewed. Never did he show any resentment that I received more invitations than he did.

My most important contribution to ministry may simply be to be a woman in ministry; to be one of those who opened the way for others to think it is possible for a woman to be a pastor. I try to work hard to make my modelling a good thing, with the help of God. I trust that in the future women will not have to work so hard to prove themselves, but simply be the best they can be. I hope that people will not need to focus on gender when they hire a pastor.

With retirement only a few years away, I have lately given thought to what that may mean. At extremely busy times, I have thought of just relaxing and being free of responsibilities. The closer the time comes, the more I realize that I will still want to be involved in ministry, perhaps less intensely, whether it's working in a soup kitchen, doing an interim pastorate, or mentoring individuals in their spiritual journeys. I have been very happy co-pastoring with my husband. If God gives us health and strength, we may choose to do something together.

Alma Coffman

"Just before I entered the Church, they asked me what I would do about my Mennonite identity. I said, When I get old, I will sit in my rocking chair praying the rosary, and proclaiming to all the world that I am Mennonite."
—A. C.

Alma Coffman graduated from Associated Mennonite Biblical Seminaries in 1976. Earlier she had trained as a nurse in Virginia, and then worked for several years in Petoskey, Michigan. Alma became the pastor of the Ottawa Mennonite Church in September, 1976, and she served there until May of 1978. Then Alma's life journey took a different direction. She joined the Catholic Church and for the past twenty-five years Alma has been at Madonna House in Combermere, Ontario. Since she was travelling through Toronto recently, she agreed to meet me at the Toronto bus depot on a stopover during her trip to Elkhart, Indiana. When I arrived at the depot, I found Alma visiting with some Mennonite people from Virginia! In my meeting with her, I found that Alma values her Mennonite roots and faith in many ways. Her story is interesting and unique, and I am grateful that she is willing to share it with us.

On November 3, 1978 I decided for sure to become Catholic. As I sat in the little upstairs chapel at Madonna House, Combermere, my emotions somehow felt almost as dark and heavy as the damp, dark, cold November night. In the silence I prayed for guidance, wisdom, and courage to know how to live out the step I was about to take.

My life was deeply embedded in the life and faith of the Mennonite Church. I had been given too much trust to turn and act in a spiritually irresponsible manner. Why would God be asking me to leave the Mennonite Church where I had found faith so profoundly? How could I leave being a pastor in a congregation, called to the proclamation of the Gospel, and my deep involvement in the Mennonite Church? As I walked down the stairs to the dining room there was peace in my soul. But how could I ever start to let those I was responsible for, and my family and friends, know of my decision: the very thought of this brought deep emotional pain, sadness and grief.

I was born into a Mennonite family on a farm in Rockingham County, Virginia. My birth was a time of joy for the family, which already was composed of three boys and two girls. Four years later another brother was born. Yes, I was a wanted baby girl, and I proved to be a happy one. My first years were lived in a world of wonder. My family included me in all their enjoyment of flowers, trees, birds and animals. We looked to God who had created the world to provide us with rain to grow the crops.

Faith in God was part of the environment I lived in. Even though as a child I was still unbaptized, I was taught that God loved me, and I didn't need to fear if I died when I was young. For me God was a loving heavenly Father, and I loved Him back. Since we were pacifists, we depended on God and the angels to protect us from harm. The Mennonite

Church community provided the environment in which I lived and looked out on the rest of the world.

When I was eight years old I raised my hand at a revival meeting meaning to indicate that I wanted to become a Christian. I was a little young, but since I seemed to understand what I wanted, I was allowed to prepare for baptism. On October 3, 1953, I was baptized at the Pike Mennonite Church. There I was in a pink cape dress, white covering with white strings, black stockings, and black shoes. The next day was the communion service. One must be spiritually prepared by being in "right relationship with God and fellow men." It was a very solemn occasion.

On a warm summer Sunday evening all the family had gone to church, except for my mother and me. I took a walk down to the pasture and stood on the pond bank. As I stood there, it seemed as if God was saying to me that He wanted me to serve Him all the days of my life. I was happy about this. I thought it meant God wanted me to be a missionary nurse. The fall of 1964 found me entering as a freshman at the Rockingham Hospital School of Nursing. It was that year a friend gave me *The Imitation of Christ*. I liked it and was surprised that such a good book could come from the Catholic Church. The morning of my graduation from nurses' training I took a walk in the woods. I stopped and sat down, and the thought came to my mind that I needed to see the world, that I had to find out what life was really about. I had to explore the options. Was there a God or wasn't there? In my journal I wrote that I had decided not to be a missionary.

I left Virginia to move to Petoskey, Michigan where I worked in intensive care and coronary care at the hospital there. Since I was working the afternoon shift, I started attending the Sunday morning service at the Petoskey Mennonite Church, but I was still very much exploring the life and culture outside of the Mennonite Church. My spiritual struggles were far from over. At work and in my social life, many people did not know that I was Mennonite. Although I wanted to use the church as a haven from the storms of life, I didn't want to be too deeply involved. It seemed to me that I had enough energy and desires in life that I didn't need God to direct it. I was afraid He would only get in the way. During all this, the pastor and his wife offered me hospitality that encouraged endless conversations over endless cups of tea.

Since I wanted to complete a B.S. in nursing, I went to Goshen College intent on going to Alaska for adventure when I finished. By chance I happened to encounter the campus pastor. During a conversation with him, he encouraged me to turn my life over to God. After a time of immense spiritual battle, I asked him to pray with me. Now the question was, 'What did God want to do with my life?'

In 1971, I went to Haiti for three months of study experience. I was assigned to the extreme north-west part of the country. Each day as I saw the extreme poverty of the country, I prayed about what God wanted for my life. How could I best serve God to help suffering humanity? Surprising to me, the idea formed that I needed to know the Scripture better. After a summer of working in a hospital in Petoskey again, in September, 1972, I went back to Indiana to start my studies at the Associated Mennonite Biblical Seminary in Elkhart, Indiana.

The planned one year of study stretched into four years as I completed the M. Div. program. This whole experience was so very rich in studies, spiritual formation, and friendships. The professors not only taught the Scripture and the work of the church, they lived it out in relationship to the church and their students. Readings such as the "Second Vatican Council" and courses in Early Church history and theology enlarged my vision of the Church. At that time I was unable to take the Homiletics course because a woman was not able to preach in churches in the area. Instead I took an internship year which included preaching in another geographical area.

When I graduated from seminary, I was invited to be pastor at the Ottawa Mennonite Church in Ottawa, Ontario. In late August of 1976, I went to Ottawa to get settled in before my pastoral duties would start on September 12. A Catholic couple, friends in Petoskey, had given me the address of Madonna House at Combermere, and of their house of prayer in Ottawa. As a brand new pastor I knew I would need to pray. At that time there were no other Mennonite churches or Mennonite pastors in Ottawa nor for many miles around. I knew I would need something for spiritual support and renewal. I decided to look up this house of prayer. Meanwhile I was installed as Pastor of the Ottawa Mennonite Church. This was to be for a three-year period with an evaluation and recall after the first year. I was not ordained, but given the permission by the congregation to perform all the functions of an ordained minister, and I was registered with the government to perform weddings. I believe that the Ottawa congregation still has not ordained its present pastor.

I started the brave task for which I didn't feel brave, that of being the pastor in a Canadian city. The idea of a house of prayer persisted in my mind. I walked the streets in the Byward Market section of the city intent on finding this Catholic prayer house even though it didn't really make sense to me to do so. After all I was Mennonite—an Anabaptist deeply committed to our history and doctrines as a unique part of the Christian Church. Finally I found the short street of Parent, and Madonna House, but a sign said they were away at Combermere. Sometime in October I returned and was invited in with a welcoming smile. Doreen showed me around, and at last showed me the chapel. I don't know why, but I knelt down in front of the Blessed Sacrament and cried. I asked if I could come back, and was assured of a welcome.

At the Mennonite Church someone pointed out to me the several books we had on St. John of the Cross and St. Teresa of Avila. I was told about Jean Vanier and his writings, so I read them too. Gradually I found myself using other books by Catholic authors. In fact, the day came that as I prepared for a sermon I realized all books on my desk, including my Bible, were Catholic editions.

My friendships branched out in other directions too. I was soon invited into a group of women involved in pastoral work in the city. We were a mixed group of Presbyterian, Baptist, United Church, Salvation Army, Quaker and myself, a Mennonite. We met together for prayer every month or so. Several times a year we would go to an old farm house in the Quebec countryside for a retreat. The Salvation Army pastor and I became close friends. Our late night phone calls when our duties were finished were a great support.

In 1976 the Ottawa Mennonite Church was considered a unique mixture of all kinds of Mennonites, including the (old) Mennonites, General Conference and the Mennonite Brethren. As the only Mennonite Church at that time in the city, we provided a spiritual home for people from all Mennonite backgrounds who chose to come. As everyone in Ottawa was a transplant from somewhere else in Canada, I also learned to know more about the broader Mennonite experience. I learned to appreciate the jokes told in low German. I couldn't understand the language, but I loved the deep, heartfelt way the people laughed. I saw the faith which was driven deep into their souls. Many people were involved in some type of government civil service, and there they lived out their faith.

My visits to Madonna House, Ottawa, continued on a regular basis. The two women there prayed with me and offered me a place for spiritual renewal. Slowly, as I asked, they told me things about the Catholic Church. I was very free to say what I believed as a Mennonite. I was so secure in being a Mennonite that my greatest identity besides being a woman and a Christian was that of being Mennonite. However, one night when I was fast asleep, I awoke with this prayer on my lips— "Holy Mary, Mother of God, pray for us sinners." Well, I was certainly surprised and perplexed! I felt a deep call to prayer. In fact, I prayed night after night for almost a month. I wondered if I was going insane. How could I, as a Mennonite pastor, do something contrary to the teachings and practices of the Mennonite church? I didn't know who to talk to about it. I certainly didn't know how to explain it to any Mennonite.

As it became more evident to me that I was being led on a different spiritual pilgrimage than my congregation, I decided to resign. I gave a six-month notice which ended on April 30, 1978. Before that, in early winter I returned to AMBS for the ministers' workshop. With friends there, I talked over my idea of going to spend some weeks or months at Madonna House, Combermere, to learn more about life in community and prayer. I was encouraged to go, and I arrived there on May 1, 1978. I have slowly gotten used to looking to the Catholic Church as my home. Just before I entered the Church, they asked me what I would do about my Mennonite identity. I said, "When I get old, I will sit in my rocking chair praying the rosary, and proclaiming to all the world that I am Mennonite."

It has been an interesting journey this past eighteen-plus years. In 1981 I took first promises as a member of Madonna House. In 1988 I took my promises "forever." I am deeply grateful to God for giving me this call to become Catholic, and to have the vocation to Madonna House Lay Apostolate. Our foundress, Catherine Doherty, will certainly stand as one of the great spiritual figures of this century. I came to know her in the last years of her life, and her writings are a constant inspiration to me. As I sometimes pray, "Thank you, God, that I was born a woman and raised a Mennonite. Thank you that I am Catholic and have a vocation to Madonna House."

Bertha Miller Landers

"When I had the privilege of being a pastor, there was the opportunity to engage the congregation in discussing and experiencing the richness of worship."
—B. M. L.

Another woman pastor in the early group of pioneers is Bertha Landers. Bertha began as a co-pastor at Bloomingdale Mennonite Church in 1980 working together with Orland Gingerich, an older pastor near retirement. Bertha became the sole pastor at Bloomingdale in 1982, and continued to pastor there until 1992 when she retired. She was licensed in 1984, and ordained in 1987. Bertha has written a number of articles for church papers, and has published a book on worship.

I learned to know Bertha while we were both studying at Waterloo Lutheran Seminary. The two of us took some courses together, and occasionally went skating at the nearby rink in the park. Bertha brought her creative gifts to ministry, and I clearly recall a nephew's wedding which she conducted. Bertha was known for her creativity in worship, and her concern for authentic worship. She says that her most significant contribution in ministry was to shape and enrich the worship experience; in fact, to teach members about worship. Bertha reflects on her experience at Bloomingdale:

Peace as an integral component of the gospel, faith lived and shared in community and articulated in service, beliefs expressed in daily living—these things I always knew would draw me to make the Mennonite Church my home. Yet there were experiences that did not, for me, embody the gospel that I read. My father, attracted by the peace stance, chose to become a Mennonite, but was always considered an outsider; he was not an ethnic Mennonite. My mother had been excommunicated for wearing a hat, rather than a "bonnet," while in California. Women missionaries who preached when home on furlough gave a "report" not a "sermon," and were thanked for their "talks," even though they preached in many churches in foreign countries. They were often assigned a mid-week or Sunday School time. Women had no voice, yet it was they who taught the children, cared for the sick, made food for the potlucks, and sewed for relief. Not only did women have no voice, we were instilled with the concept that to be born female was somehow sinful.

Another very significant observation, from my point of view, was that worship could provide much more of the spiritual dimension of wonder and mystery and allow more fully for the awareness of the awesome privilege of encountering the whole God, in community, and with our whole being. The worship service often seemed to be a word-oriented business meeting with a chairman or master of ceremonies. My expectation was that worship could comprise both the horizontal (usually a very positive component in Mennonite congregations) and the vertical dimensions, and be inclusive. Inclusive refers to worship of the whole God with our whole being, and includes all ages, races, economic groups, female and male in our language, leadership and images. The scriptures are rich in images of God, yet so often we confine ourselves to one or two only.

Since inclusive worship was not part of my experience in the Mennonite church, it came as quite a surprise to be invited to be the pastor at Bloomingdale Mennonite Church. I was also surprised to have the inner call of my youth, which I had starved and dismissed as being absurd in a masculine world, affirmed without the addition of "It's too bad you aren't a man." When I had the privilege of being a pastor, there was the opportunity to engage the congregation in discussing and experiencing the richness of worship. I was blessed with being part of a congregation that was open to looking at new concepts, was not afraid of change, and was willing to study. Those interested in leading worship, as well as others, gave of their time to attend workshops on worship. Sunday School classes also explored the meaning of worship. The congregation found that a well-planned, inclusive worship service can be a deep spiritual experience and, paradoxically, can allow for spontaneity. Worship became central in the life of the congregation and in daily life. Together we discovered that authentic, inclusive worship sends the worshippers out empowered to live as joyful "little Christs."

One simple yet memorable event illustrates an effect of inclusion. On a Sunday morning a young couple could hardly wait to speak to me after the service. The father held in his arms his daughter who was not quite three years old. This was their story: The father and their daughter were looking at the clouds and when the little girl remarked, "God's up there. That's where She lives, isn't it?" The father replied, "Yes, that's where He lives." After several such exchanges, and with the girl becoming more insistent, the father at last agreed, "Yes, that's where She lives." As the parents reflected on this conversation, they realized that the child would not have the struggles of identity and exclusion that the mother and her contemporaries faced; the child had internalized that she was made in the image of God!

To help empower people to be all that God intends them to be is something I see as part of the task of the pastor. Sharing responsibility and leadership, seeking consensus and unity as led by God's Spirit, contributes to the enabling of members to reach their potential as whole persons.

In Retrospect

In the stories of these five women, there are some recurring themes which emerge. They speak about a lack of role models, but with their creativity they found some excellent models and new ways of doing ministry as women. There were some irregularities in the procedures for licensing and ordination. Both the women pastors and the churches did not have much information about the usual procedures. Although Mennonite church policy at the time would have allowed for the ordination of women, some Conference leaders were reluctant to move ahead. It was a big step to have women as pastors in a few Ontario Mennonite churches, and leaders seemed timid about providing the credentials for women pastors, although they did help to place them in congregations.

Possibly the attitude of some male pastors who came into ministry in the 1970s had a bearing on this theme. They preferred not to be "set apart" by ordination. As a result, in the 1970s commissioning to a certain church or setting for ministry was used for a time instead of ordination. However, the commissioned status may have allowed the freedom for at least two women to be given credentials in the early days. Whatever the factors and reasons involved, the path to ordination was generally not smooth or straightforward for the first women who served as pastors in Ontario Mennonite chuches. It is my conviction that women are well-suited to the pastoral role as it has been performed in the past, and women also bring unique strengths and ways of going about ministry. Some of these have already been identified as creativity, attention to relationships, and resilience. I hope the stories and responses from the first five women, and from the other nineteen women, will demonstrate these and other unique contributions of women pastors. I am well aware that the male leaders and pastoral colleagues who encouraged and shared our ministries also demonstrate some of the same strengths. However, I continue to believe that women pastors have a unique contribution to make in the churches where they serve.

The names of certain churches emerge from these stories: Avon Mennonite in Stratford, Bloomingdale Mennonite Church, Stirling Avenue Mennonite in Kitchener, Ottawa Mennonite Church and Welcome Inn in Hamilton. While there is no clear pattern, these churches have usually continued to have women serve as pastors, either on a team or in interim situations. Stirling Avenue has had a woman as one of the pastors almost all of the time since the 1970s. Most of these churches have experienced the ordination of a woman pastor too. Certainly, members of these congregations experienced the ministry of these women as much as they were willing to accept it. On the whole, women pastors were well received and affirmed in their new roles in these churches. In a real sense the churches involved have pioneered as well.

Trailblazers

Doris Weber

Avon Mennonite Church 1974 to 1984 Commissioned/Ordained 1979. Interim Pastor Listowel, 1986-87; Brantford, 1988-89; Waterloo North Sep-Dec, 1991; Valleyview (London) 1992-93; Mannheim 1995-96; Danforth (Toronto) 1997-99; Bloomingdale, May-August, 2001; St. Mary's Hospital chaplain 1989-91. Retired 2001. M.Div. AMBS 1986 Advanced Standing in C.A.P.P.E. 1988.

Martha Smith Good

Chaplain, Mennonite Hospital, JaJunta, CO 1973-74;
Assistant Pastor, Oak Grove Mennonite Church, Ohio 1974-76;
Pastor, Stirling Ave, Kitchener 1977-79; Guelph 1981-87. Ordained 1982; Campus Pastor, Goshen College , Goshen, IN 1988-96;
Interim Co-Pastor, Lombard Mennonite Church, Lombard, IL 1998-2000;
Pastor, Warden Woods (Toronto) 2000-present; M.Div. AMBS 1974.

Doreen Neufeld

Co-Pastor, Welcome Inn, Hamilton 1976-1989. Ordained October 19,1980; Minister of Missions, MCEC 1990-98;
Co-Pastor, at Trinity Mennonite Church , Calgary 1998 to present;
Semester at McMaster Divinity College, Hamilton; M.Div. AMBS 1990.

Alma Coffman
Pastor, Ottawa Mennonite Church Sept. 1976-Apr. 1978; Member, Madonna House Lay Apostolate 1978-present; M.Div. AMBS 1976.

Bertha Landers
Director of Drama Troupe and Readers' Theatre in area churches for CGC in 1970s; Pastor, Bloomingdale Mennonite Church 1980 to 1992; Ordained 1987; Retired in 1992; M.Div. Waterloo Lutheran Seminary 1983.

Pioneers

"Along with the pain and stress of change, there is evidence of God at work through the hearts and hands of these early women pastors."
Mary Schiedel

The first five women pastors led the way for other women to serve in Ontario Mennonite churches. Several of the first group of pioneer women pastors, and some in this second group, were in leadership positions within the Conference from 1975 - 95. They served in Christian Education, on the Personnel Committee, as Conference Ministers, and as Missions Ministers. The fact that so many women pastors were involved in Conference leadership positions is evidence that men working in the Conference were willing to accept them and to work together with them.

Some women had served earlier in pastoral and leadership roles. In Toronto Helen Brenneman, Salome Harrison, and Mary Reesor gave years of their lives to Mennonite mission work. Louida Bauman served in a deaconess role at First Mennonite Church in Kitchener. As time passed, women moved into other leadership roles. In St. Jacobs, Eva Martin served as a minister of education for some years. At Hillcrest Mennonite, Nelda Yantzi Kropf was the first woman to be congregational chair. It is interesting to note that in many churches women began to serve as ushers too. They also frequently served as elders.

Women with training for pastoral ministry were also serving as chaplains in the 1980s, but the scope of this book is limited to women pastors who served in Mennonite congregations in Ontario for at least two years or more. However, I have included the names of women who have done chaplaincy in the final list of women in ministry at the end of this book. We are also including the names of young women who were youth pastors and the churches where they served. While that list is quite long, we may still have missed some persons who could be included.

By the early 1980s other women were pastoring in churches as well—some of them being licensed. Following several years of service with MCC in Zaire and two years at Seminary, Mary Mae Schwartzentruber became part of a team at Stirling Ave. Mennonite Church in Kitchener. Helen Reusser was serving as the Conference Christian Education minister, and later on she was ordained at Mannheim where she served with her husband Jim. Doris Gascho, who later became a pastor at Shantz Church, was chairing the Leadership Commission. Renee Sauder, who had done some of her training in Ontario, completed seminary at the Associated Mennonite Biblical Seminary in Elkhart, and was called to a church in Kansas. For the past ten years, she has been a pastor in Waterloo, Ontario. All of these women were pioneers who blazed new trails, and walked on paths not much travelled.

Helen Snyder Reusser

"I did have caring people who throughout my life discerned my gifts, often when I did not recognize them myself, and who invited me into service and ministry opportunities which I did not anticipate."
—H. S. R.

Helen Reusser was a Christian Education consultant for the Central District of the Ontario Mennonite Conference, and later served as Minister of Christian Education for the Mennonite Conference of Ontario and Quebec for many years. I recall hearing her speak, in a Sunday morning service, about the nurturing and training of children in Christian homes. Helen spoke in many Mennonite churches on Christian Education themes, and she also regularly conducted workshops on teaching methods for Sunday School. In her story she talks about becoming a co-pastor with her husband Jim, and relates some of her experiences in leadership in the North American Mennonite Church.

Among my greatest joys and surprises has been the confirmation of my gifts by men in leadership in the church. When I led worship at the joint meetings of Mennonite General Assembly and the General Conference of the Mennonite Church in Bethlehem, PA in 1983, I was the first woman to be given this opportunity. After leading the service, people met me in the hallway to greet me and thank me – men friends from my college days at Goshen, men leaders from our Ontario conferences and denominational leaders. I received appreciation for my style of leadership, especially that I was never pushy or aggressive. I simply used my gifts to the best of my ability when I was given the opportunity.

I had no female pastor model to follow, but I did have caring people who discerned my gifts throughout my life, often when I did not recognize them myself, and who invited me into service and ministry opportunities which I did not anticipate or ask for. My parents and my church, Stirling Avenue Mennonite, were important influences in my early Christian development, along with two female missionaries, one who went to Columbia and one to India. These two women, who gave reports to the church during their furloughs, and several others at Stirling, encouraged my interest in Christian service. I had a strong desire to follow Jesus Christ from the time I was young. Two other verses of Scripture (NRSV) which have been important mottoes for me are the following: "Therefore be imitators of God, as beloved children, and live in love, as Christ loved us and gave himself up for us, a fragrant offering and sacrifice to God." Ephesians 5:1-2 "Do your best to present yourself to God as one approved by him, a worker who has no need to be ashamed, rightly explaining the word of truth." 2 Timothy 2:15

When we were called to Mannheim in 1976, Ralph Lebold, who was then conference minister, told Jim and me that his sense was that Mannheim was not ready to credential a female pastor, but that they were ready for us to come as a team and that I could serve in any way I felt comfortable. This I did, teaching, preaching, serving on committees, visiting, serving always as a member of the pastoral team, and attending church council meetings.

By 1983 reports in the church-wide media were referring to me as "co-pastor of the Mannheim Mennonite Church." I was concerned that this misrepresented both the church and me since I was not credentialed, so I called this to the attention of the elders. Their response was, "We should ordain you." After substantive process, including preaching, teaching and prayer, as well as discernment meetings, the church came to consensus to ordain me. During this process, Herb Schultz, who was then Conference Pastor, said to me, "If Mannheim does not ordain you, Conference will, since you are the Conference Minister of Christian Education."

I had to do much praying and soul-searching before I could agree to be ordained. My husband Jim said, "Long ago you felt the call to enter Christian Service. Now the congregation is calling you. How can you say 'No'?" I was ordained at Mannheim in August of 1985. At my ordination, a number of people from Stirling Avenue, my home congregation which Jim had pastored from 1963 to 1976, said to me, "We should have ordained you when you were at Stirling Avenue." I felt much affirmation of my call to be a pastor by many people, male and female. I chaired the Wilmot Ministerial Cluster and also the Perimeter Ministerial Cluster. I have had the opportunity to preach at a number of MCEC churches, usually on Christian Education themes.

After Jim and I retired from Mannheim in 1995, we spent a year at Crosshill Mennonite Church. Jim was called as interim pastor, and although Crosshill had never had a female pastor, the congregation welcomed me to function with Jim in every way, attending elders' meetings and church council meetings, preaching, initiating a regular children's time, and with Jim, visiting every home.

My most significant contributions to ministry have been in the field of Christian Education, within many churches in Ontario, and also at Mannheim Church as co-pastor. I introduced and encouraged newer methods of teaching, especially of children. For seven years I helped to promote children's camping in Ontario as a member on the Committee on Retreat Experiences. With Maurice Martin I co-authored *In the Midst of the Congregation*. While I worked for the Conference, I produced "Nurture Nuggets," a booklet for Sunday School teachers with ideas for creative ways to teach, suggestions for activities, a list of books and resources. I also wrote articles for The Mennonite and other church papers.

What has empowered me? My inner sense of God's call, the strong support of my husband, the affirmation of individuals and of the church, and the nudgings of the Holy Spirit. I felt affirmed as I saw persons make decisions for Christ, grow in their Christian lives, and learn to use their God-given gifts in the church and elsewhere.

In regard to my image of my ministry: I am, first of all a trained and experienced teacher, and a pastor-teacher of teachers. An important part of my calling has been to support teachers and parents, and to help them upgrade their teaching methods.

These words of Jesus, the great teacher, have been formative for me, "A disciple is not above the teacher, but everyone who is fully qualified will be like the teacher." Luke 6:40 NRSV

Secondly, I see myself as a shepherd (pastor) leading and nurturing people toward spiritual maturity and toward sharing with others the love and grace of God which they have experienced. I have had a special concern for families. Jim and I shared, in at least thirty-five churches, how family worship can be creative, using examples out of our own family's experiences. Our theme was "Stand still and consider the wondrous works of God." Job 37:14.

Since retirement, I have continued to have opportunities to preach and lead children's time in a number of churches, as well as to serve on committees for Waterloo North Mennonite Church, where we now attend, for Hidden Acres Mennonite Camp, and for Mennonite Church Eastern Canada on the Senior Services Committee.

Mary Mae Schwartzentruber

"As I reflect on my years as a pastor, I believe what still surprises me the most is that I experienced a call to ministry, and that the church has been confirming it ever since!"
—M. M. S.

Mary Mae Schwartzentruber began pastoring at Stirling Avenue Mennonite Church in Kitchener, and was one of the Ontario women pastor pioneers. She was a co-pastor there, but later she also was the sole pastor of the Nairn Mennonite Church. At present, she is working as the Minister of Missions out of the office of the Mennonite Church Eastern Canada. Recently I have been working as a Mission Assistant, and have enjoyed more contacts with her. Mary Mae writes about her call and her early experiences in ministry in her unique, refreshing way.

It was 1972. I was studying full time to complete a Bachelor of Arts degree at Waterloo Lutheran University after some years of part-time studies as an elementary school teacher. This year brought me my first deeply relational, prolonged exposure to Christians other than Mennonites, since I had only recently stopped participating in the Conservative Mennonite Fellowship of my family. I remember it as a refreshing, invigorating time, with one big question always in the background: "What would God have me do after I graduate?" Since I had assumed from childhood that teaching was my lot in life, it is unclear to me how "the question" originated, but this was my constant prayer as the year evolved.

In the late fall, a representative from Mennonite Central Committee came to a chapel service at Waterloo Lutheran Seminary. Even though I had already joined the Listowel Mennonite Church, and had started teaching adult education classes, I had not yet learned about MCC—so it was delightful to discover the Teachers Abroad Programme. This was the answer to my earnest prayer! I immediately requested an application form from the MCC Ontario director, who was a bit taken aback at my certainty. "Do you wish to teach in a French speaking country or English-speaking?" How would an oral French teacher answer that? "Zaire or Haiti?"

"Where is Zaire?"

"It used to be the Belgian Congo."

No doubt - "Zaire."

By January 1973, I was accepted into Teachers Abroad Programme—and I began to tell my Inter-Varsity Christian Fellowship friends about my plans. "You are going to be a missionary?" they responded. Obviously they didn't understand the difference between MCC and mission (a difference that years later is much less clear to me). No, I was going to continue as a teacher, only this time, overseas!

If people could think of me as a missionary, perhaps they could think of me as a minister. Of course, that is somewhat of a *non sequitur.* It is not really logical, but it is exactly the thought that came to me. The fact that I had never seen nor heard of a woman minister in the Mennonite Church didn't enter my mind. In my childhood years in conference churches, I had known women missionaries. But in 1973, was it complete naiveté or denial that didn't give any consideration at all to gender? On the flight to Europe, I remember telling my MCC seat mate that when I returned to Canada, I would become a minister. He listened kindly, without comment.

In my three years abroad, I remember learning about Associated Mennonite Biblical Seminary through MCC personnel who had studied there. I recall reading with joy in one of the Mennonite magazines about Emma Richards' installation as a pastor. Years later she reminded me that I had written to her at that time.

On my return home, I recall the warm welcome the congregation offered me, the opportunity to play a variety of lay leadership roles, including teaching a newly-formed "mixed class" — that meant men and women studying together in adult education. I also recall that a young man in the church, interested in pursuing pastoral ministry, was occasionally asked to preach. I teased the chair of worship, "Does one need to wear slacks to church to be invited to preach?" I was asked to speak.

The day that I first indicated my plans for the future to my family is still vivid in my mind. We were driving somewhere when I casually announced that I intended to study at seminary for a few years so that I could be considered as a candidate for ministry in the Mennonite Church. My dear mother, who had intuitively been so in tune with my work in Zaire, fell temporarily into shocked silence. What had been my background dream for several years, overshadowed by the overseas experience in the foreground, was quite a surprise to her. Our family, divided for years by various interpretations of how to live faithfully, faced yet another divisive issue. I am eternally grateful for the quiet encouragement offered by my mother, others in my family, and many in the congregation.

In 1978, my first year at AMBS, one woman student interviewed other women about how they saw their future role in the church. Perhaps there were about fifteen women studying for credit at that time—spouses of students could audit classes, so there was a greater female presence than this number reveals. After completing her paper, she told me that I was the only one who claimed the intention of becoming a pastor.

As a single person I couldn't afford to study in the U.S.A. for more than two years, and so by the beginning of my second year I was wondering what path God would open. Imagine how I felt in spring, when Stirling Avenue Mennonite Church, Kitchener, Ontario, telephoned to invite me into dialogue about team ministry with Vernon Leis, longtime friend! Martha Smith was about to leave a pastoral role there. How I thank God for Vernon's suggestion to the Search Committee, and for the incredible opportunity to minister at Stirling!

Perhaps pioneering is one of my most significant contributions in ministry. My very being helped create a new set of images for Mennonite children—images that, twenty years later, we take for granted. I remember one little girl's eyes as she stopped drawing and colouring to watch me and to listen to my preaching. Hopefully, she would never experience the tears that came to my eyes for many adult years whenever I listened to a woman preach clearly, powerfully, and with dignity.

I remember hearing an amusing story about the eldest daughter (only five or six years of age) of a Stirling family; she used to "play church" with her two younger brothers. She was the preacher. The next child, a boy, was the organist, like his father. Unfortunately, the younger brother had no leadership role. The church secretary had to be a girl!

I felt especially called to encourage women in leadership—not necessarily, and certainly not exclusively, toward pastoral ministry; but perhaps as simply as voicing their opinions in business meetings, thinking of standing for elected leadership positions, learning to say "no," advancing their education toward personal dreams . . . daring to look beyond! One of my favourite biblical stories was that of the bent-over woman healed by Jesus so that she could stand straight and tall (or small, however she was) and look into the eyes of her neighbours and into the glorious skies!

I thank God that the church has repeatedly confirmed my call to ministry. At times I am still surprised that Christ and the Church can make use of my loaves and fishes, fallible as I am.

Doris Gingerich Gascho

"Ordination gave me a sense of the congregation and Conference and God's blessing on the work I had been doing. It was a very celebratory occasion."
—D. G. G.

Doris Gascho worked on the Pastoral Leadership Training Board from its inception in 1980 to 1986. She also chaired the Personnel Committee of the Ontario Mennonite Conference from 1981 to 1984. I met Doris first in that setting when I was interviewed before being licensed. I appreciated the warmth and genuine interest she brought to her work. Doris took seminary training and then did a Student Experience in Ministry at Shantz Mennonite Church where she later became a pastor for seven years and was ordained in 1991. There she was a pastor to some of my family, and I am grateful for her ministry to them, and to my mother in her old age, and at the time of her death.

Doris served as a Conference Minister Assistant part-time for four years. Later on, from 1994 to 1998, she was the Conference Minister for the Mennonite Conference of Eastern Canada. By the time Doris retired, many women pastors had benefitted from her work with the Leadership Commission, and also from her pastoral care. Doris is married to Ivan Gascho and has three adult daughters and seven grand-children. In relation to her ministry, Doris has written:

I didn't understand a lot about the work of the Holy Spirit until I entered pastoral ministry. The Spirit was there before that—perhaps often unrecognized. Occasionally, I had an overwhelming sense of being held and loved, often for no particular reason. It felt as if I was being loved in every pore. I wonder if Mary felt some of that "pore" love when the Spirit came on her and she became pregnant.

What people sometimes heard in sermons was not always what I had said. It seems what they heard was what they needed to hear, and I got the credit—although I did remind God, "I didn't say that, You did and Thank you!"

The Spirit was a voice at my left ear, frequently with words I should speak in a counselling setting or a congregational conflict setting; sometimes it was clearly, "Don't say that." Meaning, a thought I had that I was about to express. There were times I knew information no one had told me. It was often something I needed to know to deal with a specific situation. At other times, the Spirit spoke addressing a difficult situation where I needed to phone or visit. Occasionally, that knowledge didn't need to be used in any way; it simply gave me peace and understanding. These are but a few examples of how the Holy Spirit gave presence and assurance during the hardest work I ever loved.

Ordination gave me a sense of the congregation, Conference, and God's blessing on the work I had been doing. It was a very celebratory occasion. I enjoyed sharing the day with people I'd been working with, with my own family, the Shantz congregation, and with friends. It gave inherent validation in a formal way. Licensing, while significant, was temporary.

Ordaining and licensing other women was part of my job as Conference Minister—being a participant and offering blessing and validation for their ministry. Representing Conference in that was both humbling and an honour for me, and was a powerful experience. It was a special joy to be a woman pastor empowered to ordain others. People of various theological perspectives attend the public service of ordination. I often thought of the varied perspectives represented as I validated a woman in ministry. In Ontario it has been significant for the Conference in general, and women in particular, that leadership persons in Conference were in favour of ordaining women. The Conference role in MCEC has been basically supportive.

Women pastors have brought a particular "mothering" which has given permission, even for men, to be more nurturing as pastors. This emerges partly because of traditional roles of women in caring for aging parents and children who are ill. Women are concerned about relationships in the community and on pastoral teams. Some women pastors have had a nursing background, and women pastors bring a comfortable presence and familiarity in times of illness, births, and deaths.

Women have brought creativity in a whole range of ways: more beauty in the worship setting; cohesiveness and appeal to more of the senses through banners and other visuals; children's involvement in worship has increased; the crafting of sermons has shifted from headiness to genuinely engaging the emotions; and story is important. Women know the importance of ritual, and have designed rituals to bring healing in so many kinds of situations.

I long for the day when search committees don't think only in terms of men, but of what pastors are available with the gifts needed. I also hope for a better way of making the decision around calling a pastor. When the search committee presents a candidate to the congregation, it represents a huge amount of discerning, consulting, agonizing, and prayer. Unless individuals have clear reasons not to support the Committee's choice, I believe that the candidate should be called. While some form of review of ministry is important, vision for new and better ways is needed. During a pastoral review, congregational life becomes uncertain; and then it takes time for things to get back into a pattern that opens up the future.

I hope that MCEC, with our more broadly-based acceptance of women in ministry, will find its place in the new Canadian structure. Western voices have been strong, but our size also gives us strength. I would like to see a valuing of all parts of the church. Eastern Canada has played such an important role in the church that, with the new bi-national structure, there is a significant loss for the whole North American Mennonite Church. I trust that Mennonite Church Eastern Canada will somehow continue to make a significant contribution to the broader church.

Renee Sauder

"Being called to come back home to Ontario has felt like something of a miracle after those early, discouraging beginnings."
—R. S.

Renee Sauder grew up in Ontario and began her seminary studies here. After graduating from Associated Mennonite Biblical Seminaries in 1983, she became the Associate Pastor at the Bethel College Mennonite Church in North Newton, Kansas for seven years. She then served as Co-ordinator for Women in Pastoral Ministry with the Mennonite Board of Congregational Ministries from 1991 to 1993. Since then Renee has been the lead pastor at Erb Street Mennonite Church in Waterloo. Although her pioneering years in ministry were not in Ontario, she has returned to do significant pastoral ministry here. Renee is known for her fine sermons which are well crafted and beautifully worded; her skill with language is evident in her response below.

I grew up in the village of St. Jacobs, nestled along the banks of the Grand River. As for most children in town, the river provided me with endless summer amusement – swimming, fishing, canoeing, skipping stones, and picking the wild black raspberries that grew along the river's edge. In church we sang *Shall We Gather At the River*. As a child, balancing the hymnbook on the back of the pew in front of me, I felt nourished by the words, metaphors, and stories that flowed from the hymns and the scriptures. I drank deeply from the stream of my Mennnonite tradition, learning faith, and being refreshed by the love of people teeming in that place. I found a home and a self, a life's work and love in the church, but early on I already knew that I could not be drawn into all of its currents.

I did not hesitate to choose the waters of baptism, but I remember the animated discussion the young women of our instruction class (as it was called then) had with our pastor about the expectation to wear a head covering following baptism. I was baptized, but I never wore a head covering. This was my first, but it would not be my last, experience of going against the stream.

Maybe it had something to do with seeing the church at work in so many vital ways. I absorbed the stories that young men and women brought home from their experiences in Voluntary Service, and that visiting missionaries shared through Sunday evening slide presentations. I saw how the church poured hope into people's lives and into whole communities who were parched and dry, and I knew I wanted to be part of that. I knew I wanted to be a pastor. So I began to wade into the stream, testing the waters to see if I could put my boat into the river of ministry, hoping that the river would lead me where God wanted me to go.

In my first year of seminary at the Lutheran Seminary in Waterloo, I found myself going against the stream as I sought to enter a traditionally male profession. With few role models and little encouragement I often wondered if I would ever realize my imagined future as a minister in the church. This particular year, there were three young adults from my home congregation interested in pastoral ministry – two men and myself. We met regularly with our pastor for conversation, pondering our sense of call and how we might test that call within the church, including the opportunity to preach. I remember the disapppointment of being told the invitation to preach would not be extended to me because the congregation, my pastor felt, was not yet ready to hear a woman preach. It was a moment of feeling exiled from the place that had been so life-giving. About a week later I had a chance encounter on the seminary campus with another local Mennonite pastor. He inquired about my studies and I shared with him my recent disappointment. Without a moment's hestitation he invited me to preach in his congregation. His invitation gave me the confidence to trust in the possibility that there would be a place for me in the church.

Even as I looked forward to seminary graduation in the spring of 1983, I shared the anxiety of my fellow students, wondering if we would all find placements in congregational settings. Churches in Ontario were slowly opening their doors to women, but with few positions available, it became clear early on that I would need to be open to go wherever the river took me.

My first pastorate took me to Kansas, a land of wind-filled sky. When I arrived there that first August, I wondered how I would survive the hot prairie winds that left the landscape parched and dry. Although I was young and inexperienced, the Bethel College Mennonite Church welcomed me into its midst and entrusted me with the sacred privilege of being its pastor. It was there that I was nurtured for ministry. Their patience and understanding, their encouragement and affirmation was like a stream of life-giving water for a young woman parched for hope that the church could be a place for women and men alike to be leaders.

Ten years later, I would find welcome in another remarkable congregation. Being called to come back home to Ontario has felt like something of a miracle after those early, discouraging beginnings. I have been and am still crazy enough to believe, with Ezekiel, that "Wherever the river goes, everything will live." (Ezekiel 47:9)

As a child, I knew how difficult it was to steady oneself in the current of the river. But once you learned how to find a rock large enough to find your footing, to steady yourself, to keep your balance, then you were ready to plunge in – knee deep, waist deep – and explore the goodness of the river. Come wade with me.

Gaining Acceptance

Along with the pain and stress of change, there is evidence of God at work through the hearts and hands of these early women pastors. There is evidence of God's grace extended in ministry by them to the people of these churches, and it is clear that many in the congregations were gracious to the women who ministered in their midst. Women pastors were welcomed by many of the male pastors and leaders in Ontario. Both male and female leaders in the congregations were sometimes less ready to accept women pastors, but gradually there has been more acceptance by leaders in the congregations of the women who provide pastoral leadership.

The discovery and development of gifts for pastoral ministry in places far from where we grew up is also a factor for women who served as missionaries in faraway places. In those new settings they were free to preach as well as teach, and to minister in many ways that might not have been possible in the churches where they were raised. The Stirling Ave. Mennonite Church in Kitchener had several women missionaries, and one of them, Leona Cressman, was ordained in her home congregation for service in India. These women missionaries had an influence on many of the early women pastors.

Several of the women who responded worked in Conference positions for a number of years, and some are serving there at present.

Obviously, leaders in the Mennonite Church in Ontario have been open to working with women at this level and in the churches as well. Male leaders deserve credit both for their openness to women in ministry in Ontario, and for taking some proactive measures to encourage the acceptance of women in pastoral ministry and other areas of church leadership. Ralph Lebold, Conference Minister in the 1970s, has said that, in Ontario, leaders chose to place women pastors in congregations rather than to debate the issue on the Conference floor. While that may have put the onus more heavily on the first women pastors, it seems to have helped congregations to process the issue as they were ready and willing to do so.

Certainly there was struggle at several levels. It was a struggle both for the women and people in the churches to believe that it was "right" for women to be in pastoral leadership, and this struggle continues for some people at present. It was a struggle to find appropriate settings for women pastors where their gifts could be used and appreciated. It was a struggle for some male leaders to share the privileges of pastoral ministry with women colleagues. I believe that enough people and leaders were faithful to the leading of God's Spirit to allow the women pastors in the '70's and the '80's to minister in the pulpits and congregations of some Ontario Mennonite churches.

Pioneers

Helen Reusser
Christian Education Consultant/Conference Minister of Christian Education
- 1973-94; Co-pastor, Mannheim Mennonite Church - 1985-1994;
Ordained 1985; Interim Co-pastor, Crosshill Mennonite Church, 1995-
96; Retired 1996; Mennonite Biblical Seminary, Chicago - 1951-52.

Mary Mae Schwartzentruber
Stirling Avenue Mennonite Church, Kitchener 1980-1990; Ordained
on May 16,1982; Pastor, Nairn Mennonite Church, Ailsa Craig 1991-
97; Interim Pastor, Waterloo North Mennonite Church 1997;
Interim Executive Secretary MCEC 1998-99; Minister of Missions MCEC
September, 1999 to 2003; M.Div. AMBS 1994.

Doris Gingerich Gascho
Pastoral Leadership Training Board Staff 1980-86; Chair, Personnel
Committee Ontario Mennonite Conference 1981-84; Co-pastor, Shantz
Mennonite Church 1987-94;   Ordained in November, 1991;
Interim Pastor, Nairn Mennonite 1986-87; Conference Minister, 1994
to retirement in 1998; Studies at Waterloo Lutheran Seminary 1986-94.

Renee Sauder
Assoc. Pastor, Bethel College Mennonite Church, North Newton, Kansas 1983 – 90; Ordained March 17, 1985;
Coordinator for Women in Pastoral Ministry, Mennonite Board of Congregational Ministries 1991 – 93; Pastor, Erb St. Mennonite Church, Waterloo 1993 – 2003; Waterloo Lutheran Seminary 1980 – 81; M. Div. AMBS 1983.

WOMEN ON TEAMS

"In most of the larger congregations in Ontario, and in several smaller ones, pastoral teams have included men and women. Having a woman on the team has allowed people to have a choice, and also to benefit from the gifts of both men and women as their pastors. Many women pastors began as part of a pastoral team."
—Mary Schiedel

By 1990, ten women pastors had each served several years, and then been ordained. It is the practice in the Mennonite Church that the congregation usually recommends to the Conference that a pastor be ordained after about two years of being licensed for ministry. Most of these pastors were still the "first" women to serve in their churches—an honour and privilege to some extent, but not altogether free of pain. Muriel Bechtel, Mary Burkholder, Eleanor Epp-Stobbe, Karen James-Abra, Doris Kipfer, Sue Steiner, Jan Steckley, Ann Weber-Becker, Ingrid Loepp-Thiessen, and myself were part of this second phase. When I was ordained in 1987, I believe I was the sixth woman pastor ordained in the Mennonite Conference of Ontario and Quebec. That year there were five women pastors ordained. The licensing and ordination procedure had become more regular for women as well as for men.

Many of these women served on pastoral teams, and usually not together with their pastor husbands. In the earlier years there were such husband/wife teams, both officially and unofficially. As more women began their ministry, they became part of teams of two or three. A few women served on a team in a different congregation from the one in which the husband pastored. Occasionally, I was asked what my husband did—or whether he was a pastor—and sometimes people were quite surprised when I said that he was a businessman. Most women pastors and their male colleagues had to make some adjustments as they worked together in a team. Fortunately in the early years there was considerable flexibility as the women and the congregations grew to appreciate and trust one another. Job descriptions were important, but flexibility was also a significant factor in making things work well.

Pastoral teams have included men and women in most of the larger congregations in Ontario, and in several smaller ones. Having a woman on the team has allowed people to have a choice, and also to benefit from the gifts of both men and women as their pastors. Many women pastors began as part of a pastoral team. Some were mentored by older male pastors close to retirement; others were youth ministers who shared some broader ministry with a full-time male pastor. Most of us preached regularly in the churches where we served.

Mary Hunsberger Schiedel

"For me, ministry has been a growing experience. God opened doors, and I had to grow in faith and confidence to move through them."
—M. S.

For women in pastoral ministry, I believe the personal sense of call has had to be very strong—at least up to this time. It has been needed to give us courage to take first steps toward training for ministry, and to accept opportunities which opened up for us. The "call" has sustained us through the difficult times and during periods of transition, and of simply waiting. In their responses most women speak about their call, either directly or indirectly. The emphasis in this book is on the work we've been able to do, and how our inner call sustained us and expressed itself in the work God and the Mennonite Church called us to do. A call is unique to each person, and I write about my own "call to ministry" as a piece of the whole picture of women in ministry in Ontario.

I am told that I talked at a very early age, before I knew enough to keep quiet at certain times or places. My mother would remind me to be quiet in church, and I would promise to do that. But not long into the service, I would forget and start talking out loud. It may or may not have been an early sign of calling, but I do know that words and language have always been significant to me. More seriously, a basic part of my call was my childhood home and family. Our farm was located right beside Shantz Mennonite Church, and that congregation was an important part of our family life. My father served as a deacon there until he died at the age of fifty-six, and my mother and my older brothers and sisters were actively involved in the congregation.

Looking back has been one way for me to know how God has been leading in my life, and I found myself doing that when I first experienced some nudges toward a new form of ministry. My experience in a different setting, when I taught English at a girls' secondary school in Kenya, was a time when my eyes were opened. I helped a student worship committee plan for the Sunday morning English worship services, and for the brief, daily chapels. These services were compulsory, and were attended by all three hundred plus students and by teachers and staff members. I took my weeks of leading chapel services along with other teachers who were willing to do so.

For Sunday mornings, we invited guest speakers in to preach and to lead the longer service. Some guests were teachers from other schools, or local pastors. One Sunday our speaker cancelled fairly late in the week; and so, on Saturday afternoon, I went to visit the local retired Presbyterian minister to ask him if he would be able to come. He had another commitment, but he looked at me and simply said, "Why don't you take the service?" I don't know what I replied, but I went home and prepared to lead the Sunday morning worship. After that I did it more often, and was occasionally invited to speak at other school services in the area. In hindsight, that was a part of my calling into ministry—especially into preaching!

When I returned from Kenya in 1971, I was considering a change of vocation. The change I made was to marry George Schiedel, a widower with three sons. I very quickly discovered that not all the challenges in life were across the seas! Shortly after my marriage, I became a member of Wanner Mennonite Church. My family and members of the church were a support to me in my adjustment to the role of mother of a teenage family. Our pastor, Herb Schultz, and the small group George and I belonged to were also helpful to me. Since I was interested in doing some further study, I took several courses in counselling and social work, but then decided that I wanted to study the Bible and theology.

About that time I sensed a call to pastoral ministry. It came during an interim period between pastors at Wanners when I chaired the worship committee and was part of an interim pastoral team. I applied to go the Lutheran Seminary in Waterloo the next year, a decision I shared with a group from Wanner Church who gave me their encouragement. My husband had encouraged me earlier when I had told him about my interest in becoming a pastor. He said that he could see me doing that, although it was something his mother had never told him could happen! We had one more son, born before the older sons left home. When we planned to move to Elkhart for my final year of seminary studies, we were a small family of three. I enjoyed my experience at A.M.B.S., and graduated in the spring of 1985. Although thirty years ago I didn't dream that I would be called to be a pastor, I have been surprised at God's leading, and at the opportunities I have had to do ministry.

One of the Scriptures that has been important to me in relation to my call is Hebrews 5 in which Jesus is described as a high priest who was able to sympathize with the weaknesses of human beings. It encourages us to come to God "To find grace to help in time of need." My understanding of that was that I could receive grace to help others as well as myself. I have at times thought that women pastors have much need for grace in relating to others who are not very accepting of our work, or who are simply thoughtless. In my ministry I was often aware of my own need for grace, and sometimes only too aware of the need to be gracious even when it was awkward or difficult. From several other women pastors, I have learned that there are times when it doesn't work out well in some congregations, and that those experiences are very painful for the pastors involved, and for the churches too.

God called me to ministry through the person I was created to be, and through experiences and people who touched my life. I'm thankful that I was encouraged in ministry at Wanner Mennonite Church, and in my first interim pastoral role at Preston Mennonite. I'm grateful for the training provided by the Conference and seminaries. I appreciate the opportunities I have had to minister at Elmira Mennonite Church, and at Hillcrest Mennonite Church in New Hamburg. I was both humbled and honoured to be called as a pastor in these congregations. For me, ministry has been a growing experience: God opened doors, and I had to grow in faith and confidence to move through them.

For my first two years, I worked as a pastoral intern, a full-time job which allowed me to experience all aspects of a pastor's work. I found, as I had during my seminary training, that I could both do the work and enjoy it. At Elmira Mennonite Church, the internship was a post-seminary programme which had included a number of male seminary graduates over a period of about fifteen years. It was a great opportunity for me to learn and grow in all aspects of ministry as previous interns had done over the years. While that internship was reviewed, I was invited to stay for several additional years. Around that time, seminary internships began to take place before graduation.

Somewhere along the way I have learned to live into the future. As I reflected, I came to realize that one time I did that was in preparation for my ordination. After my first year at Elmira, I had a review of my work which also included a question about my continuing for two more years. After that helpful, basically positive review, Herbert Schultz, our conference minister at the time, suggested to the church leaders at Elmira, that it would be appropriate to ordain me. This idea startled me at first, but with the encouragement of those leaders, I agreed to move ahead toward ordination.

For me, the biggest question was the commitment to longer term pastoral ministry. I wasn't sure I was ready for it, and I also wondered where that could take place, but I decided to move ahead in faith. Part way through the months before my ordination, I realized that the experience might also be positive for the congregation. They had helped a number of interns to seriously consider ministry as they also learned more about it. So if I were to stay for several years, it might be good for the congregation to ordain me. Accordingly, we chose to have the ordination in the Sunday morning service as the whole congregation could be involved better that way. I was ordained at Elmira Mennonite Church in May of 1989. It was an experience of celebration and commitment for me and also, I believe, for the congregation.

My sense of call and its public affirmation have been part of what has sustained me in ministry. In that service, I remember another pastor saying that since God had called me, God would also enable me in ministry. The affirmations of other colleagues and church leaders were empowering for me. It was also important for me that most of my family members and friends, along with many of the people of the Elmira congregation, were able to be present at my ordination. Since then, both in Elmira and in other places, my life has been enriched by the many people who trusted me and invited me into their lives.

Pastoral care was a significant part of ministry for me during the years when I was a pastor. In hindsight, I see it as the way I earned my authority as a woman minister. Often after visiting the sick or sharing in someone's pain or grief, I would feel my sense of call renewed. When I was asked to share some of my memories of the Elmira Church at the time of its seventy-fifth anniversary, I thought of an older couple I had visited there, and recalled how our relationship had grown. Menno and Almeda lived on Union Street in Elmira when I first visited them. Menno had Parkinson's disease and they didn't get out to church at that time, so they were on the list of people the pastors visited occasionally. I learned to know them better when Menno had surgery a number of times, mostly to help keep him as mobile as possible. As I visited and prayed with Menno before his surgeries, I became aware of his deep faith in God.

Menno was human enough to admit some of his doubts and fears at times. After surgery to straighten the fingers of one hand, he felt strongly that it was enough! He was beginning to feel like a guinea pig, and had lost patience with more attempts to set things right. Almeda and the family agreed with him. Unfortunately, some further essential surgeries had to be done. One day when I went to visit Menno, he said, "I'm at the end of my rope!" Although deeply discouraged, he agreed to have anointing for healing. That brief service, held in his hospital room with some elders and family members present, was a time which Menno later referred to as significant. It had given him courage and hope. Although I was not aware of it at first, Menno had strong views about women in ministry: he was not in favour! However, over several years of illness and surgery, he did change his mind. Menno was gracious and honest enough to tell some others and myself that he now knew a woman could be a pastor. His family also knew about his changed view, and they talked about it with me at the time of their mother's funeral.

When I left Elmira Mennonite Church, I felt as though I had a crazy job. After working to build relationships, and sometimes also learning to care for people as I knew and understood them better, I had to say goodbye to many good friends. I realized that I was simply not capable of relating to more and more people as I went to minister in another congregation. A real sadness for me was the awareness that I no longer had the freedom to go into the homes of the Elmira congregation as a pastor; I needed to give up the privilege of ministering to them at times of need. I also knew that I would miss their friendship and support.

In my second assignment at Hillcrest Mennonite Church, I felt more at ease in ministry. The job description attracted me as it had pastoral care of seniors as a large component along with preaching and other responsibilities. The congregation had done some processing of the issue of calling a woman pastor, and were looking for a woman to work half-time along with a full-time pastor. As I occasionally reminded myself, I did not have to prove myself so much anymore. I recalled a friend who went canoeing with me one time saying, "You can paddle really hard if you want to, but it doesn't get you there any faster." Good advice about ministry too!

My story connects with the stories of other women pastors in Ontario in many ways. Martha Smith Good's doctoral thesis worked with the stories of six women pastors in Ontario in the 1980s. She invited us to share our stories and to meet as a group occasionally. It was an empowering experience for me. That group, with some changes in membership, continued to meet about once a month for several years.

I have belonged to other support groups over the years and some of them have included men. I have enjoyed working together with both men and women as part of a team. I very much appreciated the encouragement, support, and sense of fairness of Ray Brubacher at Elmira and of Maurice Martin at Hillcrest, colleagues with whom I worked long-term.

Although I chose to retire from pastoral ministry at the age of sixty, I have found significant ways to continue to serve. I have taken some training and have done some spiritual guidance with both men and women. I have supervised several men and women who are training as pastors, and I have been a mentor to a number of women who were beginning in ministry. I continue to preach occasionally and to lead groups in retreat settings. I have written the church history of Shantz Mennonite Church where I attended as a child. I expect to do more writing and to minister in some surprising ways in the future.

One of the humbling things about ministry is that God works through our weaknesses as well as our strengths—through our humanity. At Hillcrest I felt that the people were especially accepting of me with all of my foibles and idiosyncrasies. One clear memory I have is from my farewell service. They chose to have many of the families—especially with young children—bring a candle to the front of the church, They lit their candles toward the end of the service, and gave them to me to take home. Those candles lit my life for a year as I burned them one by one. They knew I loved candles, almost to excess.

My theology has developed in relation to pastoral ministry. I recall becoming aware of some incongruity in my pastoral prayers when I used "Our Father" as the primary way of addressing God. While I do sometimes use that way of starting a prayer in public, I began to say "Our Gracious God" most often. Later on while doing some reflection on how my view of God has changed over the years, I noted a profound shift from seeing God as All Powerful and distant to viewing God as Gracious and present with me and others—especially at times of difficulty or despair.

Recently I celebrated my sixty-fifth birthday. As I get older, I experience God as Compassionate and Wise, as Almighty and Gracious, and as both "Immanent" and "Other than human." I keep growing in my understanding of God, but am constantly reminded that I am human, and "My ways are not God's ways." I come to God for guidance and direction as well as for loving acceptance and compassion. Even in retirement I believe that life is a "becoming," and I hope to continue to grow so that I can respond to new experiences in positive ways as I get older.

Male/Female Pastoral Teams

Twenty years ago I said that the pastoral ministry in the Mennonite Church has become a multi-faceted and demanding task requiring specialization in some areas. Yet, in a profound sense, it is still the same task that Jesus had in his ministry on earth. He is still the ideal for ministry: a model that is beyond human attainment through degrees of training or specialization. Yet people are called by Jesus to ministry and to leadership and they are wise to get some training. While ministry is the task of the Church as a whole, I was concerned with leadership, and with the model of team leadership as a viable option in some of our churches. I was also interested in the contribution that women make on a team. This current writing project records the contributions made by twenty-four women pastors, many of whom have been part of a team ministry.

Over the years there have been women pastors serving with their husbands. One of the first of these was Doris Weber who was commissioned, together with her husband Rod, at Avon Mennonite Church in Stratford. Hugo and Doreen Neufeld pastored at the Welcome Inn in Hamilton. Helen Reusser worked with her husband Jim at the Mannheim Mennonite Church. Elsie and Delmar Epp, who ministered together in western Canada, now pastor the East Zorra Mennonite Church. At Nith Valley Mennonite Church a younger couple share a joint full-time position. They are my pastors, Hendrike and Matthew Isert-Bender. Since 1990 Enos and Doris Kipfer have pastored together in London with the Agape Mennonite Fellowship. Also in London, Young-Jee Na and Young-Ho Park are co-pastors of the Korean group of the Valleyview Mennonite Church. In the case of some other couples, both are pastors, but they work in different congregations.

Helen Reusser writes about the team experience: "After pastoring in a male-female team I am convinced that this is the most effective way to lead a congregation. Some persons relate more easily to a female pastor and others to a male pastor. Some issues can more easily be addressed by a pastor of one or the other gender."

Doris Weber comments on struggles which arise out of co-pastoring when the interpretations and views of each personal conflict: "The demand for understanding and compromise are a vital part of the task. The plus side of pastoring together is that two views may enhance the issue or task."

Some women worked with their husbands on a team during the 1980s and 90's, and do so at present. Because other women were serving on teams or in ministry on their own, I believe that it has helped some pastors' wives to assess their own gifts for ministry in a new way. While working together must put additional stress on a marriage at times, it also allows for more support and sharing of ministry. It is usually wise to have separate job descriptions that are shared with the congregation so that each person's gifts are clearly and fairly used. For a well-differentiated couple such a process should not be a problem. It also gives the congregation more freedom as they work with their pastors.

A few women joined an older, experienced pastor who was close to retirement and who was willing to work with the congregation in the accepting and nurturing of a woman pastor. Orland Gingerich worked with Bertha Landers at Bloomingdale for several years as she began as a pastor there. Sue Steiner began ministry in that kind of team, but has served on a variety of teams and in different settings in the years since then. Sue Steiner and Renee Sauder are two of the women pastors who are currently serving as lead ministers in their congregations. This is an area in which we need to move to greater acceptance of women as leaders.

I believe that team ministry calls for maturity and openness. Team members need to be able to share and appreciate the strengths and weaknesses of each other. By now I know that not all teams work well and there can be considerable pain involved in the sharing of pastoral work. Most teams that do function well together go through some rough times, but are willing to persevere. When they do so, they are rewarded by a "sharing of the load" in ministry, which is healthy for everyone involved.

Julianna (Julie) Bender

"The greatest surprise and disappointment for me in ministry has been to find greater faith outside the church, at times, than inside the church—although in reading the gospels, I see that this also happened in Jesus' day."
—J. B.

Julie has served with her husband Phil in two churches in Ontario. Julie had come to Hillcrest Church while I was a pastor there to speak about her experience as a missionary teacher in Ghana, where she and her husband had completed a term. They enjoyed their experience so much that they returned to Ghana recently for another brief term of teaching

After Julie and Phil Bender moved to Zurich, where they served as co-pastors at the Mennonite Church, I met Julie a number of times at Conference events. We also attended classes together to train as spiritual directors, and met occasionally on prayer days or at meetings related to spiritual guidance. Since she and Phil were called to Hamilton Mennonite Church, Julie has continued to co-pastor and do ministry in counselling and spiritual direction. Julie Bender was ordained at the Hamilton Mennonite Church on January 9, 2000. Julie shares some of her experience as a pastor:

My most comfortable role in ministry is as teacher, companion, and guide with the goal of Colossians 1:28: "To proclaim Christ" and to present everyone "complete in Christ." The image that empowers me is that of a host, welcoming and inviting people to "taste and see that the Lord is good." I have worked at this in my preaching, teaching, counselling, and spiritual direction. I feel a strong passion to invite people to trust the ultimate goodness of God, despite emotional baggage that can cause all of us to respond to a harsh, demanding God on the emotional level.

For me, the greatest surprise and disappointment in ministry has been to find greater faith outside the church, at times, than inside the church—although in reading the gospels, I see that this also happened in Jesus' day. This "greater faith" has often been found in working with marginalized persons in the community who were able to acknowledge their needs, struggles, and/or pain honestly and thus recognize their need to rely on a Higher Power. In ministering to a community person with a chronic emotional illness, we were reading about the well-watered tree in Psalm 1. This woman responded, "But what if I feel more like the petrified forest?" I found her honesty refreshing and enjoyed responding to this kind of openness.

My husband has been my strongest advocate, affirming my gifts in ministry. When he was being interviewed for his first pastoral position, he suggested that they might want to consider me for my strong one-on-one ministry gifts, and that we would offer more diverse ministry gifts if we worked together as a pastoral team. They responded enthusiastically that they had initially hoped for a husband-wife team, which was a confirmation of a call I had never seriously considered. Until then I had worked in ministry in other settings, but had never seriously considered pastoral leadership.

My most significant contribution to ministry has been to open the church doors wider, to offer a welcome and to break down the barriers between outsiders and insiders. Currently I feel led to do more one-on-one ministry—either as a spiritual director or pastoral counsellor. I have also been developing a strong interest in ministering to the spiritual seeker outside of the church. My dream job would be to work as a chaplain to the workplace.

I am sad that the Mennonite church has not been more affirming of the gifts of evangelism in ministry. I believe there is a great need to share the good news of the gospel with integrity in this post-modern age and to develop creative, non-traditional ways of growing and being the church.

Doris Kipfer

"I continue to be amazed by how openly people share and allow me to walk with them through difficult times. Their trust, and seeing the deep feeling of family and reliance on God, are my greatest joys in ministry."
—D. K.

Another woman pastor with a strong concern for mission outreach is Doris Kipfer. She uses her gifts to relate to people who meet in groups or for worship as part of the Agape Fellowship in London. Occasionally, I would meet Doris Kipfer at Conference events and we would chat for a while about ministry. I enjoyed these conversations. Recently, I have worked with both Enos and Doris as chair of a Reference Council for Agape Fellowship which they pastor together. Doris has shared the part of her life experience relating to ministry.

In 1989, I was surprised when Alvin Roth, a well-known church leader in London, included me, along with my husband Enos, in his invitation to work with and succeed him in ministry with the Agape Fellowship. I was hesitant about ministry because of my limited education and experience. One of my thoughts was "But I am a woman!" It seemed as though God answered with a chuckle: "Do you think I don't know that?" The Agape Fellowship and Mennonite Conference of Eastern Canada, affirmed the invitation and Enos and I were licensed for ministry on February 3, 1990.

House church groups, and a small worshipping community using space at a Women's Shelter, have been the focus on our ministry. Recently the Agape Fellowship has moved its Sunday worship time to several rooms at the Canadian Mental Health building. Our church family has included those somewhat marginalized because of a variety of disabilities.

In this setting I continue to be amazed by how openly people share and allow me to walk with them through difficult times. Their trust, and seeing the deep feeling of family and reliance on God, are my greatest joys in ministry. "Sharon" moved out of London several years ago, but she still occasionally calls long distance to connect and say thank you. It is a joy to see people make good changes and new discoveries, even though those changes often happen slowly. For others, progress simply means hanging on, not giving up. Some of the most painful times have been when people have given up, going back to past addictions or other unhealthy lifestyles. Others continue to create crises for themselves and others. However, we do see the enormity of the struggle. The impatience and misunderstanding of those who cannot comprehend what the struggle is about is also painful.

It has been a challenge to set boundaries around when to help and when to back off. My position is part-time, so having good boundaries for family, home, self, and another part-time job can be a challenge. It is also easy, while pastoring with my spouse, to allow the church to consume too much of the focus in our relationship. Stretching experiences continue to teach me more about the issues the marginalized deal with. This also keeps me going in ministry, as I meet and feel a bond with others concerned for the needy.

What have I been able to contribute in my ministry? Probably simply "being there" and trusting that Christ's presence somehow comes through. "We have this treasure in earthen vessels." What is my vision? I wonder how to pass on the torch for urban ministry where there is much room and need for women pastors. Although I am frequently called the "pastor's wife" (and once also jokingly, "Reverend Mother!"), I have found little resistance to my role as a woman pastor. I simply do what I am called to do. Perhaps others have paved the way so that I can do so.

Sue Clemmer Steiner

"I have attempted to lead teams in such a way that draws out the gifts of each team member while honouring the job descriptions that the congregation has designated."
—S. C. S.

Sue Steiner has served as the lead minister of the Waterloo North Mennonite Church since 1998. Earlier she pastored at St. Jacobs for eight years. In that setting I learned to know Sue, and to value her as a colleague and friend. Sue has also ministered in two churches as an interim pastor. In response to my questions, Sue comments:

Increasingly, my image is of myself as a spiritual companion to the congregation—one who tends the communal soul of the congregation as well as individual souls. I've taken the concept of spiritual direction of individuals and applied it to spiritual direction of a congregation. At Waterloo North, at the end of each meeting of our Ministry Team or our Church Ministries Council, I ask this discernment question: "Where is God in our midst?" At times of struggle, I ask "Where is God calling us as leaders-to-be in the midst of this struggle?"

What has surprised me most in pastoral ministry is that I can do it! Where people have experienced my ministry it has generally been well accepted. My most significant contributions in ministry could probably be better defined by people who have observed me in ministry over time rather than by me. However I can identify:

a) Heightening the emphasis on individual and corporate spirituality in the congregations I've served, and beginning to understand what it means to tend the communal soul of a congregation.

b) Forming ministry teams that honour and draw out the gifts of pastors and laypeople, men and women, thus leading and ministering in partnership with others.

c)This one becomes more and more significant as I get older: being a role model at a distance or a guide at closer range to younger pastors—especially, but not only, women—and to adults of various ages and of both genders who are nurturing a call to ministry.

At this time my call is leading me to pass on the perspectives I've gleaned over the years—especially on congregational spirituality and ministry partnerships—while also being open to receiving new insights and different perspectives from younger pastors and congregants. I am being led to find the synergy in leading together as older and younger ministers in an environment that is increasingly post-Christian and post-modern with more generations in the church nurtured in a different environment than I was.

My vision for younger pastors is that both gifted women and gifted men may hear the call to pastoral ministry and follow it; that they may continue to find ways of working together in partnerships that will be mutually supportive, and above all, good for the life of the congregations they serve.

Renate Dau Klaasen

"My spouse and I each bring unique strengths into the equation that neither would want to do without. The decision to minister together has turned out to be a good one for both of us individually, as a couple, and as a family."
—R. D. K.

Renate Dau Klaassen is one of a group of younger women who have begun serving quite recently. Renate is working together with her husband Randy as a pastor at the Bethany Mennonite Church in Niagara-on-the-Lake, Ontario. They pastor together as a team and see their gifts as complementary. Renate grew up in St. Catharines, and so in a sense she and her family moved back home several years ago. Randy and Renate are the parents of two children: Lydia, fourteen, and Daniel, twelve. Renate tells the story of her journey into ministry in an interesting and open way.

I am one of those women who always had a vague desire for serving the church in a spiritual way. I did not have any role models in my childhood to even conceptualize the idea of a woman being a pastor. I chose the way that was open to me: I married a pastor! By that time,

1984, some of my peers with whom I had studied at Canadian Mennonite Bible College were finding their ways as some of the first women in formal leadership positions, but I didn't feel ready for that.

We settled into a large congregation in southern Manitoba where my husband, Randy, served first as assistant and then as leading pastor, and I participated in a lay capacity in a whole variety of roles from music to teaching to some pastoral caregiving, mostly in informal ways. When our two children were small, I pulled back from some roles, and picked them up again as I was able. Still, the nudgings of the Holy Spirit and the affirmations of close friends kept me looking ahead toward some kind of formal co-pastoral work with Randy in the future.

In 1997 we left that congregation and activated our plan of spending at least one year at Associated Mennonite Biblical Seminary before seeking another congregation. I devoted that year ('97-'98) to taking courses that especially offered equipping for congregational ministry in worship and spiritual nurture, and to discerning my future as co-pastor with Randy. Although we had resolved not to concern ourselves with the search for a new congregation until the second term, a number of search committees who already knew of Randy's availability started contacting us. When we decided to proceed as a co-pastor team, one contact after another ended the conversation.

I started doubting the wisdom of our decision until one day when I was explaining to our then ten-year-old daughter why things had not worked out with a particular congregation we were considering. I told her that some congregations aren't as comfortable as others with the idea of a woman being a pastoral leader. In her frustration over still not knowing where her next home would be, she muttered "Well, that's just stupid! If kids know that's stupid, how come grown-ups don't?" At that moment, I realized that at the very least for the sake of my daughter, and all the future women leaders in her generation, I needed to stick with my vision.

After that, God made a way time after time until we were led to Bethany Mennonite Church here in Niagara-on-the-Lake, the daughter church from the congregation in which I had grown up. Ironic, isn't it? I am this congregation's first female pastor, but after a few initial hesitations at the candidating stage, they have welcomed and affirmed me at every turn. On Nov. 26, 2000, I was ordained, an event that I will always cherish as a celebration of their blessing, their full recognition of me as a spiritual leader alongside Randy, who had been ordained in Manitoba prior to our wedding.

I feel comfortable with that identity, together with my spouse, because we clearly see that each of us brings unique strengths into the equation that neither would want to do without. The decision to minister together has turned out to be a good one for both of us individually, as a couple, and as a family. As a symbol of affirmation by the congregation, I saved the envelope from a Christmas card we received from a church member after my ordination. It was addressed "Rev. Randy and Rev. Renate Klassen."

In many ways, I feel that pastoral identity covers my entire being, even though my pastoral work is only part-time. One of my hobbies is gardening, and I keep finding the analogy of the pastor as a gardener an inspiring image. It is my job to plant and tend, to work the soil, to scatter the seed, to water when it's dry and shelter when it's stormy, to fight off attacks of predators and diseases, to place the right plants in the right places, to divide and multiply them when the time is right, and to give away and share the abundance of my garden. However, it is God, and God alone, who makes things grow.

Anne Campion

"I have an undying passion for teens and their connectedness to God and to the church. I have always tried to give youth honest answers to their honest questions." —A. C.

Anne Campion has been a member of Avon Mennonite Church for twelve years. She and her husband Dave were the youth sponsors at Avon earlier, and they have two teenage children. In 1999 Anne was called and licensed as an Associate Pastor in that church. For several years after that I was a mentor who met regularly with her to reflect on her ministry. I found Anne to be very warm and honest about her own struggles in life as well as ministry. She is an outgoing person who has a passion for interacting with youth and young adults. Recently she became the Director of Youth Ministries for Mennonite Church Canada, and she also continues as Associate Pastor at Avon.

In 2003 Anne is preparing for ordination. She has some mixed feelings: "Is ordination appropriate for someone in the 'priesthood of all believers'?" she asks. But she hopes that as she says "yes" to ordination, it will encourage others to say "yes" to their unique calling in the church. Ordination will be a ritual joining the inner and outer parts of her faith, and it will be an act of submission to God as her leader. With her characteristic frankness, Anne speaks openly about her experience.

In ministry, I identify most with the image of the pastor as one who is set alongside with the occasional need to be set apart, rather than the pastor as one who is set over. I add this sense of myself as a ministering person to Anne the extrovert, Anne, the woman called by God, and Anne, the believer hungering for authentic relationship. I hunger for an exchange of my very being. When I've been most myself, ministry has happened. I lead by connectedness. It's disappointing when I can't relate as I really want to—when I feel set apart.

In the summer of 2001, when my new term at Avon was being processed, I wanted to share my own struggle with the congregation. I found myself asking: "Would it not be better for us to pray and discern together? Could our discernment help us hear God's desire for our congregation as a whole, and for myself as an individual seeking to be faithful to my call?" I was counseled not to do that, so I didn't; and I feel okay about that decision. But I still believe that in an authentic faith community, one person's process could help another person.

My inner call has empowered me. In this second term at Avon, God's call for me continues to be primarily with youth and young adult ministry, but I connect with the other pastoral ministries within the church and to the leadership team. An ideal for me is owning my own call so deeply that I don't need the affirmation of others to walk in ministry. A real blessing is my own sense of being centred in my relationship with God so that I can say an ongoing and free "Yes" to God, however He might call. Two passages that hold me in this are: Jeremiah 1:4-9 and Habakkuk 2:1-4.

I have an undying passion for teens and their connectedness to God and to the church. I have always tried to give youth honest answers to their honest questions. My best friend's daughter once said, "Anne, there you go again, you have to bring the God thing into everything!" In my new part-time job, I have a passion for a Church which young people and young adults will want to stay with, a church that allows them to lead us into new ways of being the church. Perhaps this is why another image of pastoral ministry I identify with is that of pastor as mid-wife. For me there is great joy in walking with young people as they discover how God is present with them, and encouraging them in their growth as leaders. I'm concerned with protection of the infant too—the vision of a younger person.

I still struggle with the place of friendship in my ministry. I have always considered myself one who easily makes friends, yet in the years since I have answered the call to pastoral ministry, what was once a wider circle of companions has been narrowing, and I have often found myself isolated and lonely. The cost of leadership has been high. I believe intimate friendships and places of support are essential to healthy ministry. While at times perilous, it is possible to have friends in the congregation to which we are called, and to be vulnerable in healthy ways. It can be a way for us to love our congregations.

The choice to remove our masks brings wonderful potential for an authentic Christian community that the world outside the church walls seldom sees! As leaders model vulnerability something happens in a congregation; members can be vulnerable with each other, they see the pastor less as one elevated on a pedestal, but more as one who is growing alongside the congregation. Pastors on pedestals have greater heights from which to fall, and fewer fellow journeyers to catch them when they need to be held in times of their brokenness. The challenge is to know when and where are the appropriate times to risk entering in, and to put into place relationships outside the congregation that help us sort things out.

Another contribution I make is my own forward vision for the Church. More and more I see myself as a visionary who sees the possibilities for a church. I'll always be the pastor who wants to go forward. But I know that new possibilities grow out of the faithfulness and teaching of the Church. It's good for me to be on a team! I have a growing sense that God is leading me to pastor in a new or beginning church. Possibly I will serve in an urban setting. God is calling me to a new post-modern church with many more people coming to faith through search and struggle. People today want an authentic community.

Team Leaders and Team Players

Sue Steiner has been a part of several teams, and she makes some significant comments on team ministry:

First of all, I do believe that teams need to be led. My experience is that leaderless teams can use up an inordinant amount of energy in sorting things out within the team—energy that would better be spent ministering to the congregation.

The teams that I have been invited to lead have included both staff ministers and lay persons with responsibilities in pastoral care and spiritual oversight. I think it is important that ministry teams include laypersons. I have attempted to lead teams in a way that draws out the gifts of each team member while honouring the job descriptions that the congregation has designated. I have attempted to share the ministry responsibilities that are "winners" with other team members, while also not "hiding" as lead minister, and not giving away responsibilities that are meant to fall to me. Ministering as a team is very important to me, and I've noticed that if a congregation where I'm ministering does not have a team approach, I attempt to create a team anyway!

Other women have been part of teams in a variety of ways. A number began as youth ministers and over time moved into a broader ministry. Julie Ellison White began as a youth minister, and then moved on. She has been the sole pastor for several months in her home congregation, and is now in her second congregation as a co-pastor in a male/female team. Julie writes about team ministry.

It is a delicate dance learning to navigate the differences in style and personality that come with a mixed-gender team. In my present team situation we have a wonderful time working together, and are doing some really proactive things to ensure we keep on this track! I feel so blessed to be in a relationship with an open, flexible team player.

My vision for women pastors in the Mennonite Church is that they might feel and be perceived as fully equal to their male colleagues, that their style which comes from ministering out of a feminine heart would be validated and appreciated. Both men and women are created in God's image and I believe the church loses something when it does not take seriously the part of that image which women, and women pastors in particular, represent. I pray that mixed gender teams might be healthy and positive experiences for all members, and that power would be distributed and used in ways that are life-giving and liberating for all.

Varied teams are present in Ontario Mennonite churches in 2003. Many of them include a woman on the team; in several churches, women pastors are the leaders of the team. Because women generally are more concerned about relationships, I think most women pastors on teams work hard to make the team function well. I have observed that a team of two may need less time for team meetings than a team with three or more individuals. In all cases it is important that the job descriptions arc clear both to team members and to the congregation. However, they may need to be re-written from time to time, and then the congregation should be made aware of the changes.

Women On Teams

Mary Schiedel
Associate Pastor, Elmira Mennonite Church 1985 – 1991; Ordained in May, 1987;   Interim Pastor, Preston Mennonite Church 1981 – 82; Elmira Church 1989 – 90; Co-pastor, Hillcrest Mennonite Church - 1991 – 1997; Retired in 1997; M.Div, 1985 AMBS. Training in Spiritual Direction.

Sue C. Steiner
Associate Pastor St. Jacobs 1987-90; Co-pastor, St. Jacobs 1990-95; Ordained on Pentecost 1987; Interim Pastor, Nith Valley 1996-97;Black Creek (Downsview) 1997-98; Lead Pastor, Waterloo North Mennonite Church, Waterloo 1998 to present; M.Div. AMBS 1982. Training in Spiritual Direction with groups and individuals.

Doris Kipfer
Co-pastor, Agape Mennonite Fellowship, London 1988-2003; Licensed 1991. Retired 2003.

Julie Bender
Mennonite Board of Missions, 1988-93; Zurich Mennonite Church 1993-97; Licensed May 17, 1993; Co-Pastor, Hamilton Mennonite Church, Hamilton 1997 to present; Ordained January 9, 2000; M.S.W. Western Michigan University, 1982. Training in Spiritual Direction.

Renate Dau Klaasen
Co-pastor Bethany Mennonite Church, Niagara-on-the-Lake 1998 to present; Ordained Nov. 26, 2000; Studied at AMBS 1997-98.

Anne Campion
Associate Pastor Avon Mennonite Church, Stratford 1999 to present; Licensed September 1999; Mennonite Church Canada Director of Youth Ministries, Feb. 1, 2000 to present; Studies at Conrad Grebel College - 1999 to present. To be ordained, June, 2003.

Sole Pastors

"Maybe it's not surprising that so few women pastors have served as the sole pastors in congregations."
—Mary Schiedel

Some women have served as the sole pastor in a congregation—usually a smaller church and one which is out of the Kitchener-Waterloo area. Alma Coffman served the Ottawa Mennonite Church for sixteen months. Bertha Landers was the first woman pastor at Bloomingdale Mennonite Church, and she was the sole pastor there for ten years. Karen James Abra served at Nairn for five years. Audrey Mierau served at Harrow for several years before her marriage to Ken Bechtel. Mary Burkholder was the pastor at the Valleyview Mennonite Church in London for four years. Beverly Suderman Gladwell was the pastor at Erie View Mennonite Church at Port Rowan for seven years. Muriel Bechtel served as pastor of the Warden Woods Church in Scarborough for almost twelve years. Catherine Hunsberger has served the Selkirk Mennonite Church since 1996, and Anita Janzen has served at Hanover Mennonite since 1998. Martha Smith Good was the pastor of the Guelph Mennonite Church for eight years and is currently the pastor of the Warden Woods

Mennonite Church. These women pastors faced some different challenges as they related to their congregations.

Mary Mae Schwartzentruber served as the pastor of the Nairn Mennonite Church from 1991 to 1997. She reflects on her experience as a single woman pastor there and earlier in relation to other aspects of her life:

> After two years of study at AMBS, I left Elkart in 1980 with a sizeable debt; and since then I've had continued financial stress as a sole wage earner due to further study and part-time ministry. As a single woman pastor for seventeen years, I dedicated my time and energy very freely to ministry. Now as a married woman pastor, there are some external boundaries on my work hours. I'm aware that someone would like me to be home for dinner! As a single woman pastor, I also remember welcoming gray hair because it seemed to me that salt and pepper hair could carry with it for my church members a little more automatic authority. For many years people's first impression was of my youth!

A number of women pastors have brought their life experiences and pastoral gifts to interim ministry. I began ministry in this category at Preston Mennonite Church for one year, and I also did an interim year at Elmira later on. Other women such as Doris Gascho, Mary Mae Schwartzentruber, Martha Smith Good, Sue Steiner, Phyllis Tribby and Doris Weber also have served as interim pastors at various churches. Usually we worked as the only pastor in the congregation during the interim. I believe that the broad life experience of those of us entering ministry at mid-life, or after retirement, also has had an impact—especially in the interim situation. The emotional aspects of going through transitions are quite familiar to women along with the demands of family life.

Doris Weber served in many interim settings with the conviction that if people experienced women in ministry some of their fears would lessen. She says, "I said I was willing to go to a church with a fifty per cent vote of acceptance as long as they would give me six months. If it was still fifty per cent after that, then I would leave with no hard feelings." In interim ministry, votes are not so common, but Doris has served wisely and well in many interim situations. When we consider interim positions, we find that more women have served as sole pastors, and that many more churches have had women pastors.

Karen James Abra

"My work at Nairn Church gave me the opportunity to develop community once again. I was challenged to help people to accept differences in theology and ways of expressing faith commitment."
—K. J. A.

Karen James Abra was one of the women pastors ordained in 1987. Karen is from the Baptist Church, but worked first as a chaplain in a project sponsored by the Western Ontario Mennonite Conference. In 1985 she was called as a pastor to the Nairn Mennonite Church. That congregation along with others from the WOM Conference is now part of Mennonite Church Eastern Canada.

I recall meeting Karen at Conference activities and sessions. At a School for Ministers at Conrad Grebel College, Karen presented a case study of the Nairn congregation that I found very interesting. It was insightful and well done. I thought the Nairn Church was fortunate to have her as a pastor. Later I was startled to hear that she had left the congregation rather abruptly, and that it was not a happy ending.

When I learned that Karen and her family were living in Stratford, I decided to contact her about my writing project. She agreed to meet with me for an interview, and graciously shared with me her experiences at Nairn, including the painful ending. I was impressed with her affirmation of the congregation in spite of her pain. Her continuing ministry of counseling and spiritual direction reveals her creativity and her resilience. Karen is still true to her calling. The following is how Karen recounts her experiences as a pastor:

In 1980, my husband and I both graduated from McMaster University with a Master of Divinity. We asked to be considered separately for placement. My husband was called to a church in London so we moved there in the fall. Wanting to use my gifts and training, I eventually contacted Alvin Roth and became involved with some of the projects he had initiated in London. Knowing my interest in community development, he encouraged me to do research for the Western Ontario Mission Board regarding the possibility of establishing a chaplaincy position in a rent-geared-to-income housing area in London. The board hired me to do the research; then, in 1982, commissioned me as chaplain in the Limberlost government subsidized housing area. I thoroughly enjoyed this opportunity to integrate skills from both my social work and pastoral training. A highlight for me was our monthly potluck supper and worship service. It was heartening to see the healing that came when people felt they could both give and receive from their own community and the churches beyond their borders. Some of the stigma attached to living in a rent-geared-to-income housing area was lessened as a result.

After some time, I was encouraged by the Western Ontario Mennonite Mission Board to seek ordination with the Baptist Convention of Ontario and Quebec since my roots were with this denomination. My husband's church, which was then helping to support the Limberlost work financially, agreed to endorse my ministry as part of their outreach work. However, the larger Baptist community was unwilling to grant me ordination. It seemed that my request to be ordained pushed at too many traditions at once: my way of describing my call to ministry was unique; the fact that I was a woman seeking ordination was difficult for them, and the non-traditional setting and the ecumenical nature of my work was different from a traditional church pastorate. The experience of having my ordination request turned down by the Baptists was disappointing and disheartening for me.

My oldest daughter Erin was born in May 21, 1984. I took a four-month maternity leave, then returned to the chaplaincy work in Limberlost on a part-time basis. At about this time, a position for a part-time pastor became available at Nairn Mennonite Church. I submitted my name and was delighted to be called as a pastor there, starting in the summer of 1985. We moved there as a family and found the congregation very welcoming and supportive to us as young parents. The church responded to creative worship ideas and were hard-working in their efforts to be a community for each other as well as for their neighbours. I soon discovered it was a church that had experienced considerable trauma in its short life: a few people had started several large community projects which taxed peoples' efforts to the maximum; several of these hard-working families moved away to establish a new church in New Brunswick leaving the remaining Nairn families to grieve their absence, and the pastor who preceded me had had an affair with a congregation member, causing heartache and disillusionment. In spite of all of this, I found that most of the members were willing to trust my leadership and to continue to work hard.

Sarah, our second daughter, was born on November 11, 1986. Doris Gascho was interim pastor during my maternity leave. On

September 27, 1987, I was ordained as pastor of the Nairn Mennonite Church by the Western Ontario Mennonite Conference. This was one of the happiest days of my life. It felt like a long-awaited confirmation of my calling. The sermon was preached by Martha Smith Good, who was my mentor for the first year of my work at Nairn. Herbert Schultz performed the ordination ceremony.

During my time at Nairn church, we worked together to develop a vision statement that continues to give the church a sense of direction. Also, the decision to build a new church was made and initial funding proposals were discussed during my tenure there. My work at Nairn again gave me the opportunity to develop community once again. I was challenged to help people to accept differences in theology and ways of expressing faith commitment. Throughout my time there, there was tension between some of the senior founding members of the church and some of the second generation families in the congregation. Some of the senior group had difficulty with my leadership because I was a woman. Their discontent intensified when it became evident that my approach to worship and evangelizing was clearly different than that of the original pastor at Nairn.

About a year before I left, two simultaneous events happened which overwhelmed me emotionally and led to my resignation. First, I became involved with an eighteen-year-old woman who came to the church and declared that she was being sexually abused by her father and that she needed refuge apart from her family. She also stated that she had cancer and needed ongoing treatment in a hospital in London. She wore a hospital bracelet and carried medication and other medical equipment for emergency use. She stayed with one family in the congregation for a time, left them abruptly, stayed with my family for about two months, then left for still another family. Each time she moved, she attempted to turn people against each other. In the end, we discovered that she did not have cancer; and in fact much of what she had told us was lies. From my experience now, I know that she was a victim of a mental disorder, but it was not until much later and after she moved to London that she received psychiatric treatment. Our involvement with this young woman was exhausting and painful and led to many unresolved feelings in the church community.

The second devastating event was the arrival in the area of a new family from the Niagara region. The husband did not believe that women should be pastors, and began agitating to have me removed from the Nairn Church. He did this by meeting secretly for a Bible study with a handful of discontented seniors from Nairn Church and a Pentecostal church leader at a Bible School in the area. Without my being aware that this movement was in process, the group gathered "evidence" over a period of about four months to prove that I was a heretic (my word). They proceeded to call the Mennonite Conference office and ask that I be dismissed. The Conference responded by organizing a meeting with those who were discontented and the rest of the church. Most of the people came to my defense, speaking highly of my work as a pastor. For perhaps the first time, the second generation members challenged their seniors to be forward-looking in expectations of Nairn Mennonite Church. The process was valuable for this reason. The man who had instigated the insurrection left the Nairn Church. However, I chose to resign in August of 1990, feeling too depleted to continue.

As I look back, I remember Nairn Church with fondness. I believe that each member was acting out of a sense of integrity. I also think that I was young, idealistic, and had limited experience in handling the type of conflict that developed in the congregation. I had a young family and had extended myself beyond my limits. We moved back to London where my husband continued to work as a hospital chaplain. I became a part-time chaplain at the Children and Parents Resource Institute while I worked on my Masters of Education in counselling psychology at the University of Western Ontario. Once I graduated, I worked as a counsellor in London at London Family Services and the London Interfaith Pastoral Counselling Centre. We moved to Stratford in 1995, and I was hired by the hospital to work in Listowel for five years as a community mental health counsellor. I now work full-time in private practice as a counsellor in the Stratford area. I miss the opportunity I had as a pastor to develop community, but enjoy the ministry I have as a counsellor.

Mary Burkholder

"I am a facilitator by nature, and so I am naturally empowered when empowering others. In my ministry I readily discovered that pastoring a congregation offers abundant opportunities for doing just that."
—M. B.

Mary Burkholder was at a turning-point in her life after serving with MCC for some years when we were both studying at AMBS. She graduated from seminary with an M. Div. in 1986, and began to explore possibilities for ministry in Ontario. After an initial testing with a congregation whose search committee decided not to take her candidacy to the congregation, Mary was called to the pastoral ministry at Valleyview Mennonite Church in London. Later Mary moved to Kitchener and served the Conference as Executive Secretary for six years. Several of us met as a support group for each other, and so we had more regular contact during those years. For that reason perhaps, Mary shares quite openly about some of her struggles in the pastoral ministry.

When I entered congregational ministry at Valleyview in 1987, there were not many women pastors as role models, nor had I ever experienced the ministry of a woman pastor in the congregation, and so I proceeded by trial and error. I think I intuitively felt that a pastor was "different" from other humans, but didn't quite know how, and so found it awkward to integrate my role as pastor with myself as female. I dressed conservatively, and tried to fill the role suitably at all times. And I did get affirmation from family, congregation, and others for my "appropriate" dress and comportment. But I denied myself much spontaneity, and I now feel I was trying to be someone I really wasn't.

Another influence on my developing sense of pastoral identity at that time was my conviction that ordination was not scriptural, and that the priesthood of "all believers" (rather than the ordination of a select few) was God's ideal as a basis for congregational life. So although I was licensed at the beginning of my pastorate, I resisted ordination. I now realize that this path did not lead to full empowerment for my ministry. And so, on a couple of fronts which now appear to be almost contradictory, I believe that God's Spirit was not fully released to affirm my personhood and to guide and inspire my ministry.

A breakthrough came during my fourth year of ministry when I participated in a very challenging Clinical Pastoral Education experience. Here my peers and supervisor helped me learn to look at and accept my shadow side. I found this a tough struggle; but at the same time I was also freed: free to stop trying to be someone I was not—free to be myself with my full package of gifts and weaknesses, and fully loved and cherished by God.

This was a powerful insight—so powerful, in fact, that I felt led to leave congregational ministry and get in touch with myself in a different setting. During the next number of years in work for the broader church, I accepted the call to ordination for "specialized ministry." Now this empowering felt important for me vocationally, although I still had some uneasiness with the distinction between an ordained clergy and "the laity." Such a distinction did not quite resonate with my inner convictions of our equality under God and the giftedness of all the congregation, but I reluctantly came to accept it as necessary for the empowerment of pastors in their ministry.

After my retirement a few years ago, my home church called me and a younger woman to lead the congregation for one year of transitional ministry. I found this call truly affirming and empowering in a way different from that of ordination. During that year of shared ministry, both of us pastors were given the joyful opportunity of offering our people our strongest gifts and thereby complementing one another. My young colleague loved to preach and plan worship, while I provided pastoral care, led in the rituals of the church like child dedication and communion, and provided administrative oversight. It was beautiful. In short, this is my truest image of ministry: when a person is called by a people of God to offer her gifts to them for the common good and for the growth of the body. And when there is a sense of others (other "pastors" and all members) also offering their gifts, so that ministry is shared in the fullest sense, and leadership is gentle and empowering of others.

What surprised me most in pastoral ministry was my love-hate relationship with preaching. When I entered seminary in mid-life after a teaching career, I chose the academic track and so by-passed the supervised preaching, although I later took it on an individual basis during my internship and enjoyed it. When I subsequently accepted a call to congregational ministry, I readily assumed I would enjoy preaching, since all my life I had done public speaking, and in seminary had learned to enjoy working with Scripture. To my dismay, I discovered during my first year that preaching—both preparation and delivery—was frequently a burden.

I now sense that some of the heaviness around preaching resulted from my ambivalence about my pastoral identity, and my difficulty in integrating my personhood with myself as pastor. This made it hard to deliver sermons with conviction and passion. I found it hard to "internalize" them—make them "mine." I would also add that I am at heart more a teacher than a preacher, and now recognize that I will probably always feel most comfortable in a teaching role. However, I was also surprised on numerous occasions when God's Spirit broke through the heaviness and breathed inspiration. I now sense that my most effective, spirit-filled sermons were those in which I was free and authentic. I recall an early sermon where I told my life pilgrimage and growth into faith using a collection of artifacts from my past. One of the youth in later years told me how that message had made a profound impression on her. My Mary Magdalene Easter monologue one year was passionately alive! And the message where I was given courage to share around my CPE experience with my shadow was life-enhancing for all, I believe. At this point in time, I still enjoy preaching on occasion— particularly on a topic for which I have a strong passion, and I occasionally enjoy opportunities for "teaching" from the pulpit.

I am a facilitator by nature, and so I am naturally empowered when empowering others. In my ministry I readily discovered that pastoring a congregation offers abundant opportunities for doing just that. I delighted to put books into people's hands that dealt with a particular issue of concern that I was aware of. I enjoyed working with the Worship Chair on themes for worship, resourcing the Christian Ed. Committee, routing broader church literature to appropriate persons, welcoming newcomers and helping them connect with others—are some that come to mind . . .

Other times of feeling God with me in ministry were experiences such as these:

—planning and leading worship which flows around a theme; in particular I recently found joy in leading congregational prayer which focuses on that theme.

—preparing worship rituals to mark milestones in members' lives, such as: finding active involvement for parents in their children's baptismal services; helping plan and lead a special small group supper followed by communion; offering healing to a couple who had experienced a miscarriage; and helping a Catholic priest plan a wedding liturgy for a mixed marriage (We came up with a wonderful blend of Catholic and Mennonite tradition. I had the privilege of being the first woman to preach a sermon in that Catholic church and to be affirmed by that parish.). A different kind of challenge, but poignant with meaning, was an intimate anointing service for a young man who felt much inner turmoil from which he yearned for release.

—conducting membership classes, both with adults and also with youth. Numerous times adults from other religious backgrounds desired to join the Mennonite faith, and I had immense pleasure drawing up and teaching a series of lessons on the Mennonite -Anabaptist faith, bringing together songs, writings, poems, and art work to illustrate the various topics. Perhaps I felt so fulfilled in these opportunities because of my previous training and experiences as a teacher.

—providing pastoral care: some of the most meaningful encounters I have had with parishioners have been those times they experienced the loss of a loved one, and I was privileged to share in their hospital vigil, accompany them to the funeral home to help make plans, and then walk with them through those days of visitation, and final committal, and the weeks following.

In my retirement, other than the one-year interim ministry, I have chosen not to seek further involvement in congregational ministry. However, I am pleased to be involved in occasional pastoral tasks as available: I continue to preach from time to time, to perform occasional marriages of relatives, to officiate at funerals in special circumstances, such as those of close relatives or friends outside the Mennonite Church; in my home congregation, I enjoy leading worship and/or offering the congregational prayer as needed or desired. In general, I value being a caring presence and listener. I include intentional "give and take" encounters with a spiritual companion. In short, I am very much enjoying the freedom I now have of selecting ministerial involvements in areas in which I feel most comfortable and declining those that I feel less comfortable doing.

Muriel Bechtel

"As women ministers, we are still functioning in the long shadows of many generations of women whose avenues for exercising legitimate authority were limited."
—M. B.

Muriel Bechtel was a lay member of the ministry team during my interim year at Preston Mennonite Church. I experienced her then as a caring, helpful and encouraging person. Recently I have experienced her encouragement of this writing project, and am grateful for her willing participation. Muriel took her seminary training at Toronto School of Theology (TST) after her family moved to Toronto, and then was called to pastor the Warden Woods Mennonite Church in 1991. After almost twelve years of pastoral ministry in Toronto, Muriel moved back to Kitchener. In 2000 she became the Minister of Pastoral Services for the congregations and pastors of Mennonite Church Eastern Canada. Muriel reflects on her years in pastoral ministry in the congregation, and also from the perspective of her present work.

My primary image for ministry has been a "coach." For much of my adult life I have thought of myself as someone who encourages and nudges and invites and inspires people to do and be more than they think they are capable of. The modeling of teachers and other adults who "coached" me to stretch and use my gifts shaped my volunteer work with co-leaders and participants in women's groups at Preston Mennonite Church, in Langs Farm Village, and continued as a theme in my life. I enjoyed encouraging others to think about new ideas, ask new questions, try new things, and talk about their relationship with God. Coaching is fun when people are learning and growing and things are going well, but it is harder when things go wrong or someone messes up. More difficult for me has been learning how to combine encouragement with challenge, how to hold together God's grace with "speaking the truth in love."

The moments when the light of Christ shines through the church and God's people, despite the darkness that threatens to put it out, do empower me. I have experienced this personally and seen it in the lives of others—times when God's people saw someone suffering and struggling alone, and stayed with them until they were able to go ahead on their own. Times when I have received wisdom and insight beyond my own understanding just when I most needed it; ordinary "saints" who in their simplicity and love for others, especially the marginalized and the "little ones," reflected the life and spirit of Christ.

An experience that inspired me, during a time when "keeping on" was hard, was a baptismal service on Pentecost Sunday during my final year at Warden. I had been leading a youth Sunday School class of four girls in a study of Ann Weber Becker's *Faith for the Journey*, based on the Mennonite Confession of Faith. When we discussed the article on baptism, one of the young women, Tessa, decided that she wanted to be baptized and join the church. As a nine-year-old, Tessa had a cancerous growth surgically removed from her brain stem. It was a delicate emergency surgery, and the whole church community prayed for her and her family as they went through this frightening experience. Two years later the tumor returned, and once more Tessa faced a risky surgery. The week before the second operation, a small group of close friends met for an anointing service with Tessa and her family. This time the surgery was more radical, leaving Tessa with significant nerve damage and many physical challenges, but also a tenacious spirit, strong faith and deep compassion for the suffering of others. Through it all, Tessa and her family were upheld by the church with their prayers, gifts of food, and support. Although life with her peers in high school was often hard, Tessa knew she was loved by God, her family and her community. I was not surprised that Tessa wanted to be baptized into this congregation.

In the week prior to the scheduled baptismal service for Tessa, Alvin, a fifty-eight-year-old Jamaican man, who had been attending the church for less than a year, came to my office to tell me the news from his doctor that he needed surgery to remove a large cancerous growth along with two-thirds of his stomach. The surgery was scheduled for the following Monday. We talked about what this might mean for him, about his previous life as a professional boxer and his estrangement from some of his family. In spite of the ominous odds before him, Alvin had an unshakable faith that God would be with him as God had been there through his past struggles. When I asked him whether he would like the congregation to pray for God's healing and anoint him with oil before his surgery, he accepted the offer gladly. Then, somewhat instinctively, I asked if he had ever been baptized. "But I'm not good enough to be baptized!" he protested. I explained to him that baptism and being part of the church were not a matter of being "good enough," but of accepting God's grace, and the support of other sisters and brothers to follow Jesus, wherever that journey might lead.

That Sunday morning both Tessa and Alvin were baptized. Their personal testimonies were brief and simple. There was barely a dry eye in the congregation as we poured the waters of baptism over their heads and welcomed them as a brother and sister in Christ. Then we surrounded Alvin, laid hands on him, and prayed for God's healing in his life as we anointed him with oil. The next day Alvin packed his baptismal certificate with his other belongings that he took to the hospital. To him it was a reminder that friends in his new community of faith were holding him in their prayers. Alvin lived another year, during which it was evident to all who knew him that God was bringing about healing in many areas of his life. Whenever he felt well enough, he was at Sunday morning worship. During coffee hour Alvin and Tessa would sit and talk to each other. Tessa visited him weekly, whenever he was in hospital, until he died. Alvin would introduce her to the nurses as his best friend.

I was no longer Alvin's pastor when he died, but my heart rejoiced when I heard how many family and friends were there to celebrate his life and faith. His new pastor, Martha Smith Good, led in worship, Tessa spoke some words of tribute, and Tessa's father, Tim, led the congregation in an exuberant rendition of "Soon and very soon we are going to see the King." It was not only Alvin who was changed. Many in the congregation and his family were touched by God's love through Alvin's faith and the way it transformed his living and dying.

Some personal experiences that have "kept me going" at various times have been those sacred moments when God spoke to me through a particular scripture, friends or a dream. These were powerful reminders that God knew and understood my struggles and was with me in them.

A particularly poignant example was during an Advent retreat in Colorado when I was feeling that the weight of my role was more than I could carry. I was reading the story of the angel, Gabriel, announcing to Mary that she would bear a son and that he would be the Messiah. As I read Mary's response, I wanted to scream at God, "But she was only a child! An innocent and naive young woman! You didn't have her 'informed consent!' How could she have known what her 'Yes' would cost her? It was not fair!"

The next day I rehearsed with a group of church choirs from the Denver area preparing for their Advent Vesper service. We learned three arrangements of *Ave Maria*. Through the familiar words and beautiful music, God re-introduced me to Mary who said "yes" to God without knowing the pain and the cost it would mean for her. Gradually I began to realize that just as God gave Mary the strength she needed, God would give me what I needed.

Being in ministry has been a growing process. Earlier in my ministry, I resisted the authority of the pastoral role, wanting to be like everyone else. However, in my present role, I am learning to recognize the power of an "office" as never before, to acknowledge when I misuse it, and to seek to use it for the good and growth of individual pastors and of the broader church. Often that requires me to be a peacemaker and mediator between adversaries and to develop a thicker skin than I naturally have. I am learning at a more profound level than ever before that leadership is not about being nice or liked by everyone. Sometimes it requires taking a position that will not be popular. I wonder if that is harder for women than men.

In my present ministry assignment as Minister of Pastoral Services, I find I am being called to a much closer relationship with and reliance on God. Daily I am reminded that I cannot do in my own strength all that is required of me. I am being called to forms of ministry that do not come easily to me. Sometimes I feel alone and bereft of the friendship of those who were previously my peers. Yet over and over I am given what I need at just the appropriate time. Paul's words are certainly being proven in my life: "My grace is sufficient for you, for my power is made perfect in weakness" (2 Corinthians 12:9).

Where this will lead me next is still a mystery. I have never set long-range goals for myself, but rather have watched with joy and surprise (and occasionally fear and trembling) as my life and ministry have evolved in ways I never could have imagined.

It seems God has called me precisely to those places where I was sure I would never go. Yet in the end God has always been faithful. I expect to approach the next stage in a similar way. Perhaps I will take an overseas assignment with my husband, or work as an interim pastor, consultant or spiritual director. It will be "unrevealed until its season, something God alone can see."

Catherine Bean Hunsberger

"I have learned that the congregation doesn't mark a pastor on each sermon. Instead they respond to the overall ministry provided."
—C. H.

Catherine Hunsberger began seminary studies while she was working as a secretary to the Pastoral Leadership Training Programme directed by Ralph Lebold. She had also done some preaching when she served as an elder at Shantz Mennonite Church. Catherine was called to be the pastor of the Rainham Mennonite Church at Selkirk in 1996. Catherine has served on the nominating committee for the North American Mennonite Church. She has also been on the task force for the restructuring of Mennonite Church Canada.

Catherine is my sister-in-law and I have enjoyed relating to her over the years. Since she has been a pastor, we frequently talk about her work, and about what is happening in the Mennonite Church in Ontario and elsewhere. Catherine has carried a heavy load as she cared for my brother who was in a nursing home for several years until his death last spring. She was a zealous provider of care for him, as she is for people in her congregation. Catherine has a young adult daughter, Beverly. I am thankful for the gifts Catherine has and which she uses with much love and integrity. She tells about her experience:

I have served as pastor of the small Rainham Mennonite Church at Selkirk, Ontario since 1996 The Rainham congregation dates back to 1793 when the first Mennonite settlers from Pennsylvania came to Lake Erie's north shore. Rainham is a small congregation, and requires only a part-time pastor. According to the search committee, the congregation wanted a pastor who would lead them. After supervised ministry expreriences at Preston and First Mennonite, Kitchener, I was ready to be a sole pastor. A smaller congregation would be a good place for me to test my gifts and also to grow as a pastor. The downside of being a sole pastor is the weekly sermon preparation routine. Fortunately, I usually enjoy preaching.

Rainham has been a good place for me to minister—in spite of the 115 kilometre commute from my home in Waterloo. While preparing for ministry, I often heard warnings that the first few months or years would be like a honeymoon, until some disagreement signified that the "honeymoon was over." I have been pleasantly surprised that mine with Rainham has lasted so long. I have found it to be an extraordinarily accepting and affirming congregation. For my sixtieth birthday, the church surprised me with a party following the morning service. After cake and ice cream, each person present said something they appreciated about my ministry.

I have learned that the congregation doesn't mark a pastor on each sermon. Instead they respond to the overall ministry provided. I do feel that my preaching is appreciated. One annual Historian's Report stated that in 2001, "Our little church was blessed with some excellent preaching." My ministry with families at times of funerals and weddings has also been affirmed. My experience at Rainham has confirmed my sense of call, and the church has grown somewhat, in spite of deaths and members who moved from the area.

My sense of call to ministry was present long before I openly acknowledged it. I worked at a local bank and helped my husband with our dairy farm, but felt that there was something else I was called to do. At Shantz Mennonite Church where my husband and I were members, I asked whether I could do things for the worship service—make a banner, do a reading or find a suitable story for Lent. Later, pastors Vernon Zehr and Doris Gascho encouraged me in various leadership tasks—chair the worship committee, lead worship and occasionally preach. Both pastors recognized my gifts for pastoral ministry and affirmed them. Before entering the M.Div. programme at Waterloo Lutheran Seminary, I needed to finish the BA degree I had begun earlier. While working on the degree, I was a staff person for MCEC.

My image of a pastor is a dredger of springs. The Rainham congregation was tired and in need of refreshment. There were no children attending. Soon after I went to Rainham, we started having a Sunday morning Bible study. We also have Sunday School for children who have started to come. We enjoy a coffee break between the worship service and the Sunday School hour. Periodically, I look at congregational life to see where direction is needed. A Leadership Team assists in this task. I believe that for a congregation to be healthy, both pastor and congregation need to attend to prayer. Organizing communal prayer has been difficult, given a full, two-hour Sunday morning, and my distance from the church.

I was licensed as a pastor when I began ministry at Rainham. To date I have not been ordained. I intended to ask for ordination in 1999, but this was postponed when my husband became ill. I also discontinued my seminary studies for three years. At present I am considering ordination which was postponed due to my care for my husband during his illness. The congregation and the Conference have been encouraging me. I hope to be ordained in 2003, and to graduate from seminary in a few years.

Anita Janzen

"Having been a bit of a rolling stone all my life, I have finally come home."
—A. J.

Anita Janzen and I met in Phoenix, Arizona at a Board of Education meeting. She attended as a representative of AMBS as she was a student there at the time. She was wondering whether there would be a place for her to serve after graduation. Since she had told me she came from Toronto, I suggested that she might want to apply to MCEC as some churches in Ontario were open to calling a woman pastor. A year later I found that she had been called to minister at the Hanover Mennonite Church. When the Leadership Commission asked me to be a mentor to Anita for the first several years, I was happy to do that, and enjoyed meeting with Anita from time to time.

Anita made the adjustment quite quickly from living and working in the big city to life in the small towns of Walkerton and Hanover. She likes preparing sermons and planning for worship, and brings energy and creativity to her work. Anita faced the challenge of living on a part-time salary, and has found additional work at times. As she now feels more settled, she looks forward to more years of ministry in Hanover. Anita reflects on her transition into ministry:

I have come into ministry late in life. I knew all my life that I wanted to be "in ministry," but did not know what that looked like for me. I spent two terms overseas and thought that might satisfy this urge. I worked in the church and held every position but two—treasurer which I did not want, and worship chair which I wanted quite badly. It was the seniors I worked with who kept saying "Anita, you should be a preacher." I would laugh and say "Not me." However, when I lost my job I had to evaluate my life and plan for the future.

I had at one time applied to AMBS, but didn't know what I wanted to do with that degree. Now I decided to test the waters. If my application was still active, if I could find financial support, and if my peer groups in the Clinical Pastoral Training unit I was planning to take would be affirming, then I would go to seminary. Everything worked out positively and in the autumn of 1995 I left for AMBS. The three years at AMBS were a time of healing for me. I had had a very difficult return from the Congo; I had been in the Eastern Congo for six weeks in a Rwandan refugee camp, which left me more traumatized than I realized. I worked hard and enjoyed each and every class I took. The staff and students were great. I graduated in May of 1998.

In September of that year, I began as half-time pastor at the Hanover Mennonite Church. I immediately "fell in love" with the congregation. That is not to say that there have not been glitches. They are the kind every pastor faces—concern about commitment, worship style, and outreach. We have managed to work well together through these concerns, but have not necessarily resolved them.

One of the more difficult things for me is being so alone in the work. Not having a spouse, or other confidant to process things with, makes ministry a little more difficult than it could be. There is no colleague ten kilometres down the road. I am not lonely, but I feel alone. I have just recently found a place that offers retreats and spiritual guidance not too far away. I intend to follow through on this.

Was it a good decision to go into ministry? Yes, definitely. A friend commented several years ago, "Anita, you have done a lot of things— which was the best?" Without hesitation I answered, "This is." Would I change anything? In a perfect world, I would be working in team ministry where I could concentrate on worship and liturgy. In a perfect world, I would move this congregation one hour closer to a larger centre. But in this world, there is not much I would change.

This congregation has been incredibly loving, giving, and supportive. They have taught me so much, and I believe I have taught them as well. Having been a bit of a rolling stone all my life, I have finally come home.

Continuing Challenges

Mary Burkholder comments on challenges which she faced as the sole pastor in a congregation: As I think back to my four-year stint as sole pastor of a congregation, I feel the greatest challenge I faced was loneliness. Since I was single, I had no spouse to turn to for emotional support; and while there were a variety of supports in place for me—a female pastor as mentor, the cluster ministerial, the local inter-faith ministerial, as well as the Pastoral Relations Committee at church, and various friends within the congregation—none of these could really pick up my deepest emotional needs and/or provide adequate opportunities for venting in safety. I suspect this is an on-going reality for single pastors. I wonder now whether I did not recognize at the time how deep-seated this need was, and so did not attempt to find creative ways of dealing with it.

The work load wasn't a major challenge per se. The congregation was modest in size, and there was a good congregational infrastructure. My job description called for me to preach only half-time which was extremely generous, I felt. However, as time went on, the congregation was hoping for their pastor to pick up more of the preaching, given the increased busyness of the "lay preachers." Since, by then, I had discovered that preaching was one of my bigger challenges, I wasn't prepared to take on more. This dilemma became a major consideration in my decision to leave that ministry. Shared ministry, by way of contrast, permits more flexibility in negotiating ways where each pastor's strengths can be utilized. For me the shape of the job, rather than the quantity of work, was the more crucial consideration.

I don't recall "authority" as a signficant challenge. My sense was that being sole pastor gave me more authority than I would likely have experienced in a shared ministry, and I valued the confidence placed in me.

Muriel Bechtel also comments on the challenges of pastoring alone: For me it was a challenge to own and exercise my authority appropriately. Sometimes in my over-zealous attempts to give leadership, I promoted my own issues or causes and did not consult enough with others who had differing viewpoints or who wanted to give priority to other issues. Other times, I was too hesitant to take action or make decisions that were needed because I was afraid of people's reactions. As women ministers, we are still functioning in the long shadows of many generations of women whose avenues for exercising legitimate authority were limited. Many of us are still learning to find that "place just right" for exercising our leadership and authority without either placating or overcompensating in the direction of exerting our authority.

The other area that I found hard was loneliness. It was not that I did not have friends as a pastor. In a way, as pastors we are in a privileged position where everyone sees us as a friend. The challenge is having friends outside of our pastoral relationships. Becoming a pastor profoundly changed the relationship between me and some of the women who had been friends, but who were now in my congregation. It is only with some emotional distance, and more experience, that I can see how my own confusion of roles and attempts to be just "one of the women" contributed to the struggles between us.

These women have identified the struggles that may stand out more clearly for women ministering alone. Maybe it's not surprising that so few women pastors have served as the sole pastors in congregations. When they have done so, it has often been part-time, and that has been difficult financially. Of course, more women than these five have served alone in churches—there were several others whose stories appear in previous sections. When we include the experience in interim ministry, about six more women would be included in this group, and the total of sole women pastors is close to fifteen. This small number, out of a possible fifty, probably indicates a growing area for churches as well as for women pastors.

I believe that many women like to work with others. Our Mennonite church heritage may also affect our choices as women pastors since the "group gathered together around God's Word" is a familiar image to us. Some women pastors enjoy doing ministry tasks and studying with others. Since the smaller church settings do offer an opportunity to work with local church leaders as a team, I think that more women could be pastors there and serve them well. In the future I hope that more churches who call only one pastor will benefit from the gifts of women.

Sole Pastors

Karen James Abra
Chaplain, Limberlost Community, London 1982 - 85; Nairn Mennonite Church 1985 to 1990; Ordained in 1987; M.Div., McMaster University 1980; M. Ed. in Counseling Psychology, University of Western Ontario 1992.

Mary Burkholder
Pastor, Valleyview Mennonite Church, London 1987-1991; Executive Secretary, MCEC 1991-1997; Ordained 1995; Retired 1997;
Interim Co-pastor, Rockway Mennonite Church, 1999-2000; M. Div AMBS 1986.

Muriel Bechtel
Warden Woods Mennonite Church, Scarborough, ON 1988 - 2000; Ordained, 1992; MDiv, Emmanuel College TST, 1989; D. Min, Emmanuel College T.S.T., 1997; Minister of Pastoral Services, MCEC, 2000- present.

Catherine Bean Hunsberger

Pastoral Intern, First Mennonite Church, Kitchener 1994-95; Pastor Rainham Mennonite Church, Selkirk 1996 to present; Licensed October, 6, 1996. M. Div. Waterloo Lutheran Seminary, in progress.

Anita Janzen

Pastor, Hanover Mennonite Church 1998 to present; M.Div. AMBS 1998.

PASTORS AND MOTHERS

"One reality is that even when working part-time as a pastor, the family or marital schedule is greatly affected by church activities, meetings, and Sunday worship."
—Mary Schiedel

Another group of women pastors is larger, and on the average younger. Most of these women have served for two to eight years and are presently pastors in churches throughout the various clusters of Ontario Mennonite churches. This group includes: Susan Allison-Jones, Hendrike Isert Bender, Anne Campion, Julie Ellison White, Wendy Jantzen, Anna Hemmendinger, Anita Schroeder Kipfer, Anita Janzen, Sherry Martin, Barb Smith Morrison, Shirley Schultz, Judy Shantz, Jan Steckley, and Anne Weber Becker. Almost all of them are licensed or ordained. These women pastors are between the ages of twenty-six and sixty-six. Their stories reflect some pain and struggle as they have moved into ministry, even though credentialling is quite routine by now. They also experienced much joy as pastors.

Coming to pastoring in mid-life meant that I had a mostly grown-up family of three stepsons, their wives, some grandchildren, and one younger son still at home. My husband was very supportive of my ministry and, since he had his own business, was able to partially retire when I went to seminary. Our older sons and others took over the business, and so he never returned to full-time work. Because he was semi-retired, he didn't always appreciate the busy schedule which pastoral work gave me, and so encouraged me to work part-time and then to retire at age sixty. At the age of twelve, our youngest son once commented that some people didn't think it was okay for a woman to be a minister, but he thought it was all right. Actually the whole family was supportive, and family times gave us a relaxed setting away from the church I was serving at the time. I am very thankful for an encouraging and supportive extended family as well. In the '70's and '80's a number of women had school-age children, teenagers, or young adults in their families. Of course there were struggles. One reality is that, even when working part-time as a pastor, the family or marital schedule is greatly affected by church activities, meetings, and Sunday worship.

Doris Weber reflects, "As a mother and wife, one of my ongoing struggles was juggling home, family, and ministry. It was a real struggle not to feel guilty about what I could not do due to lack of time and energy. There were times when I knew I could have done better and possibly been more effective if there were not so many divided interests."

When I interviewed Doris Gascho, a retired Conference Minister for MCEC, she expressed continuing concern about our younger women pastors:

The struggle between pastoring and mothering will likely continue for women pastors—especially when children are young. I don't see resolution of that issue. Karen James Abra had the first maternity leave, and I happened to be the interim pastor at her church, the Nairn congregation, when that happened. Anne Weber Becker also took a maternity leave shortly after being ordained at First Mennonite in Kitchener. Others have followed; some have returned to pastoral ministry, others have not.

Jan Steckley, who has continued to pastor part-time while bearing, giving birth, and parenting three children, shares her concerns and questions about women pastors with young families:

One of the areas I have felt a growing concern around for some time, with regards to women in ministry, is the whole issue of females pastoring while raising young families. I have noted during my years in ministry that while there seems to be openness to accepting women in ministry, women do not seem to feel that they can combine pastoring and parenting in the early years of their children's lives. Many of the young women who were pastoring before they had families have left ministry during these years. I wonder whether they will return, or if, in the intervening years, their lives will call them in other directions.

Will we lose their ministry gifts? I wonder why it is that the same issues and questions do not seem to be present for men. Is it any more acceptable for men to be out of the home during those years? I wonder what it is about the expectations of ministry that make it seem too difficult for women to find the balance between private and public life during those years. I expect that these are issues we have not yet addressed in the "women in ministry" question. I did write a paper on this subject for an Integration Seminar. I have shared it with a few people, but wonder if someone somewhere needs to name this. I still hear women getting comments with regards to where they should focus their time and energy during those years that I don't think would ever be made to a man.

I also share the concerns expressed by Doris and Jan. More women with young children have entered ministry in the 1990s, and I hope that many more young women will consider ministry, therefore I believe that these concerns need to be addressed much more seriously by our churches in Ontario. Some creative solutions have been found, and more women are co-pastoring with their husbands, but we need to look at various options. In some cases too much of the onus has been put on the husbands to be supportive, while the demands of their careers and also their individual coping abilities are varied and unique.

If we accept the calling to ministry which these women have experienced, and since we have done so and ordained them, we need to struggle with them to find wholesome solutions to their dilemma. I want to bring this issue into the open so that we can work with it more effectively. For women pastors with young children, or young women who are pregnant with a first child, these questions are crucial. We invited a number or them to share their experiences and their hopes.

Jan Steinmann Steckley

"I have often felt that one of my 'calls' has been to bring the experience of women to bear on our theological understandings— to help others to see how the experiences of women offer insights into who God is, and how God is at work in the world."
—J. S. S.

Jan Steckley began ministry as a youth pastor in her home congregation, Steinmann Mennonite Church, near Baden. She was then called to the Breslau congregation for nine years. Jan continued to pastor part-time while bearing and caring for her three sons. She was ordained at Breslau in 1994. At present Jan is the full-time pastor on a team at Hillcrest Mennonite Church, New Hamburg, where she has been serving for five years. Since I had been a co-pastor there for six years, before I retired and Jan was called, I am especially happy to see her move into ministry with increasing commitment and responsibility. Jan shares her story of growing into pastoral ministry with some refreshing comments and insights.

Probably the image of ministry which has been most helpful and powerful for me is the image of pastor as midwife. When I was pregnant with our youngest child a little over ten years ago, I was experiencing a difficult time in my ministry at Breslau. I had been there just over two years, and, because of some critique of my ministry on the part of a small group of people, I was struggling with my sense of call to ministry. During my maternity leave, I was able to find some space from the church and ministry in which to work at pastoral identity and call issues. It was a pivotal time for me, and I eventually did accept the congregation's call to another three-year term.

Soon after returning to work, I prepared and presented a sermon for Lent about the parallels between the physical birthing process and the process of giving birth spiritually. Because we had had a midwife for all three of our children's births, and because I was giving birth spiritually and physically at the same time, I was able to think about my role as pastor in those kinds of terms. A midwife is one who supports, creates a safe and comfortable setting for birth, walks with the one giving birth, and forms a birthing "team" with all others who are part of the birth process. That image has helped to bring clarity to my role as pastor and helped me to remember what the focus of my work is—to assist the birthing process.

I have often felt that one of my "calls" has been to bring the experience of women to bear on our theological understandings—to help others (women in particular) to see how the experiences of women offer insights into who God is, and how God is at work in the world. I do not see this as exclusive or over and against the experiences of men, but rather as adding to the picture, a piece which has for the most part been missing. I have sensed and sometimes been told that women appreciate hearing their "stories" in the pulpit and having their perspectives named.

Interestingly enough, I have also had a few men comment positively on having a "feminine" perspective offered. One Sunday I did a dramatic monologue type sermon on Niccodemus, and afterward a gentleman came up to me and said, "That was really good, but why didn't you share the story from the perspective of Niccodemus' wife? I think it would have been really interesting to get that perspective from you as a female."

I have also been aware at times that how I do ministry as a woman is part of my calling as well. How do my gender and my experiences as a woman affect my ministy? This is certainly not my only call, nor even perhaps the most central one for me, but I do recognize that I am providing a role model for others in a role where I had almost none.

After about thirteen years in part-time ministry, I accepted the call to full-time ministry at Hillcrest Mennonite Church where I am now pastor. When I had been at Hillcrest for two years on a half-time basis, my full-time male colleague left. As we looked at transition issues, a question began to be asked of me, "What does this mean for you?" Eventually I was asked directly by leadership what I saw my role as being or what I wanted it to be as I looked to the future, and if increasing my time was an option I wanted to consider. I think we all recognized that if I were to make any change, now would be the time.

There were a number of reasons why full-time work could be a possibility. All our children were in school full-time, my spouse was making a transition to a job which afforded more flexibility, but what eventually came clear to me was that the shift from part to full-time was not just a functional question but one of call and commitment. I realized that, as long as I was part-time, I could in some way limit my commitment to ministry because of time restraints. I began to sense that moving to full-time ministry would require a new level of commitment —the willingness to embrace my call in a somewhat new way.

Congregational leaders asked me to share something of where I was at at a congregational meeting where we were discerning what we would look for (time-wise) in additional pastoral leadership on an interim basis. After sharing, I left the meeting and the congregation worked with the issue. By the end of the meeting, they extended a call to me to accept full-time ministry for the remainder of my current three-year assignment. That felt like a significant call for me personally and an affirmation of my ministry. Now, two years later, I am living with the reality of what that call means—that I must own fully the leadership role to which I have been called.

Since Hillcrest is at a pivotal point in its life, examining its identity, mission, and vision, my leadership role continues to be an interesting and sometimes challenging experience. Some days I'm glad for the call and excited about it; other days, I'd rather the call belonged to someone else!

Ann Weber Becker

"Thus began the always interesting, often intense, and sometimes confusing interplay between my life at home and my life out there. In conversation with other women, I came to describe the interplay as a conflict between a 'public call and a private call.'"
—A. W. B.

Ann Weber Becker was one of the first younger women to train for ministry, and I learned to know her when we were both studying at AMBS. She was called to begin ministry in Kitchener, Ontario. Ann was a pastor on the team at First Mennonite Church with responsibility for youth ministry. She served there for eight years. Ann was a member of the small support group of women pastors who met during the 1980s, and we enjoyed her youth and enthusiasm for life.

Ann writes about the struggle of leaving "public ministry" after she and Byron had their second child. She chose to do some freelance work, and served on the committee which produced the draft of the Mennonite Confession of Faith in 1995. She brought her creativity to her work as executive producer of "Songs to Live By" recordings. Ann is a fine writer who wrote a column for Canadian Mennonite *for several years. She has written here about the dilemma of parenting and pastoring with courage and fresh insights.*

Releasing my infant from the still-unfamiliar car seat, I was excited. During the months of my pregnancy I had wondered when I would bring our baby to church for the first time. Now here we were, on a crisp Tuesday morning in October. The cars in the parking lot verified that this was a WMSC day—a day when many of the senior women of the church gathered to quilt, visit, and worship. The pastors of the congregation had a standing invitation to join the Women's Mission and Service Commission for lunch on meeting days. Since many of my responsibilities involved the youth of the congregation, I relished these opportunities to connect with these senior women. I enjoyed hearing their stories, and frequently left nourished by their seasoned wisdom and gracious faith.

When these women were my age, they heard many sermons about what faithful discipleship entailed and did not entail. Shyly at first, then with increasing depth and always with good humour, they had gifted me with insights about the journey from the days of head coverings and cape dresses to the days of women in pulpits. Though this congregation has been blessed with many female leaders over the decades, I was the first to be formally ordained to a pastoral role. I felt humbled and deeply honoured to have been warmly welcomed by these women as one of their pastors. Now we were on the verge of another "first": I was bringing my firstborn to meet them.

Miraculously, our son chose this morning to be wide-eyed and happy; we enjoyed wending our way through the welcoming crowd. I am sure that words were exchanged, but laughter, tears, and hugs are what I remember. We have a photo of our son being held by someone who held my father as a child, wrapped in a blanket crocheted by the hands of another. I cherish the memories of that morning.

Can anyone claim to know at the time of his or her baptism exactly what a call to follow Christ will mean? For some, I believe the answer is "Yes," or at least leaning in that direction. I have encountered persons who speak of knowing from a very young age, or at one decisive moment, the path God intends for their lives. Others I have known speak more of a journey motif: making a commitment to discipleship, and trusting God to guide as one moves through life.

For myself, the journey metaphor comes closest to describing my experience of God's call to discipleship. I was actually in a vehicle, barely old enough to drive on my own, on my way home from a church-related committee meeting, when the thought came to me: "Not everyone enjoys meetings. But I do." This insight was like a tiny spark. While my enamourment with committee work has had its ups and downs over the years, I view that solitary moment in the car to be the beginning of an adult consciousness of Christian call. The pattern of my journey since then could be mapped something like this: train the eye to recognize when God is placing an opportunity before you; pray for the strength to step into the opportunity; seek God's wisdom as you journey through the new experience; and discern how this maturing wisdom refines your call and trains your eye.

Can anyone claim to know what it will mean to be a parent? Most of the new parents I have come to know would say, "I had no idea." It is one thing to know that babies need frequent feedings and diaper changes. It is quite another thing to get up night after night, week after week, to attend to these needs even if you are sick. It is one thing to know that children will require medical attention. It is quite another thing to hold down the toddler you love for stitches, or a needle, or worse. It is one thing to know that a young child needs constant supervision. It is quite another thing to figure out how to manage that while preparing food, chatting with another adult, or using the washroom once in a while, and then the second child arrives.

For myself, parenthood came as a shock. The surprise caught me off guard. After all, I had had a lot of experience working with children in church and community settings. But neither my husband nor I had spent much time with babies. One of the biggest adjustments was realizing that the role of home in our lives had changed forever. Pre-baby, home was mostly a place to crash. We would come home to eat, to rest, to re-fuel for a life lived "out there." Of course, I shared a home with my husband, but there were many other things that we shared as well, also "out there." We had moved often in the early years of our marriage, so our sense of being at home had more to do with a relationship than with a sense of place. This changed dramatically with the arrival of our son. It became quickly apparent that the physical, social, cognitive, emotional, and spiritual home that we created for him would have an impact on the person he would become. Post-baby, "home" became nothing less than a crucible for shaping a soul.

Thus began the always interesting, often intense, and sometimes confusing interplay between my life at home and my life out there. In conversation with other women, I came to describe the interplay as a conflict between a "public call and a private call."

Conflict can be productive, and there were certainly positive sides to this one. As my responsibilities grew, I could better appreciate the juggling acts required by families to offer a high commitment to church life. The visceral grief of a miscarriage was instructive in my emerging pastoral care. I was also aware that my sermons were not the same. My young child was teaching me how to be present in the moment in ways that felt new to my intuitive, "big-picture" tendencies. Looking back, he was really a tiny spiritual guide leading me in a re-discovery of God's creation and everyday wonders. While I am unable to articulate precisely how this spiritual growth impacted my study and interpretation of the Word, I know that it did.

Juggling public and private callings also presented challenges. Many of these challenges are shared by any parent who works outside the home during this chapter of family life. While combining mothering and pastoring may not have produced unique stresses, this combination did produce certain pressures and strains. Pastoral ministry requires availability when crisis situations arise. Caring for small children is also fraught with crisis potential. In good weeks, the crises do not overlap, but what happens when they do? Pastors also need to be able to receive communication from people in the congregation. We started our family in the days before e-mail and even before the widespread use of answering machines, so there was compelling reason to answer the home phone when it rang. Learning to use an answering machine was a big help, but knowing the phone could ring in our home at any hour produced for a young mother a double around-the-clock responsibility.

My husband and I found ways to manage these stresses. Also, I was blessed to serve a congregation that was sensitive to the balancing of public and private life of all of its pastors in our various life stages. I was serving half-time. With planning, creativity, good humour, and patience on both sides, the arrangement appeared to be working for both our family and the congregation.

Still, I could not silence a niggling voice in the back of my head. The voice kept reminding me how quickly the early years of children's lives pass. I would have the majority of my life to work and serve in the public realm, but the fraction of my adult life involving the nurture of my own children in their early years would come and go. The voice also suggested that in managing the juggling of so many responsibilities, we might be missing something we did not even know we were missing.

The Lord works in mysterious ways. I was driving home from a church meeting when the thought came to me: "I could do freelance work from home while my children are small." Maybe I did not need to decide between public and private callings so much as re-envision what the combination might look like. I was on the same road that I had been driving when the "I like meetings" spark had occurred years before. The more I thought about the freelance option, the more I was convinced it could work. Even so, it would be over two years until my life was actually structured in this way.

Why did it take so long to act on this call? I quickly realized that what to me felt like a reconfiguring of two callings could well look to others like choosing one calling over another. Whether or not it was a "choice," a decision was required. The decision took a long time to make, because I felt burdened by it. To begin with, I knew that even to have a decision to make in the matter placed me among the privileged elite in the world. How many mothers wanted to be home with their children, but for lack of a stable financial base could not afford to make that choice? I also knew that while stepping out of a formal public role might simplify some challenges, it was bound to create others. I feared the potential isolation of "being at home." Would I be bored? (As I would find out, these were not idle concerns.)

At the root of the dilemma was the burden of making the decision as an ordained female pastor at a time when such a person was still relatively rare. I did not always feel like a trailblazer. My work as a pastor was to me a natural outgrowth of my God-given gifts, commitments, and academic preparation. Still, I was aware that others before me, equally gifted, never even considered serving God in pastoral ministry because they were taught that a woman's place was in the home, serving God there. Here I was, the first woman in my congregation's history called to formal pastoral ministry. How could the person in this position possibly leave the pulpit to stay home with her kids?

I was well aware of the stories of some of my older sisters in the faith in other times and places who had felt called to ministry without the opportunities to exercise those callings. I had heard their frustrations. I had felt their grief. I was acutely aware that the opportunity to serve as a pastor was a sort of inheritance passed on from an earlier generation, and I did not wish to squander this inheritance. But what was the inheritance exactly? Was the inheritance essentially an opportunity to serve in pastoral ministry? Or was the inheritance a challenge to answer honestly to the callings in one's life, in spite of potential roadblocks and misunderstandings?

In the context of continued reflection and discussion I came to believe that ultimately I was accountable to God, for how I responded to the callings presented to me on my journey. I explained this as best I could, and arranged to step out of the pastoral position at the end of my term. This decision has had both its rewards and its consequences. I hope it was a faithful decision. I know that it was a productive one, girded with the assurance of having answered a call.

One day I mused, "What if I were to make a list titled, 'Important Things I Accomplished In My Thirties'?" Certain sermons, publications, and other contributions to the public realm would be noted on the list. Also noted would be moments from the private realm that by definition never made the spotlight. For instance: hearing barely audible toddler feet announcing the end of the afternoon nap as they pad their way down the hardwood stairs. Without a word, this toddler crawls into my lap and we rock, watching the snow make its silent descent into our neighbourhood. God's love is palpable. The experience is simple, and solid. This moment and others like it did not happen by accident. It took some courage to get there.

Some day in the future, when my hair is grey and my joints have begun to feel the weather, I hope that I may have opportunity to welcome a young couple as they carry their first-born to church. I will be eager to hold their infant, and listen to them. What choices will they face as new parents, embarking on that fearsome and wondrous journey of raising the next generation in the context of their own stories of discipleship? Will my story be of any value to them? I only hope that I may receive them with as much graciousness as the senior women of my congregation received me as the journeys of our lives unfold, intersect, and sometimes take surprising turns.

Julie Ellison White

"The pastor is set apart in a special way that does not devalue the contributions of other church members. Ordination is an acknowledgment that the pastor has a central role to play in the spiritual birthings of a congregation."

—J. E. W.

Julie Ellison White was a co-pastor with responsibilities for youth ministry at Tavistock Mennonite Church during her six years there. For several years I was a mentor and spiritual director for Julie, and enjoyed my contacts with her. Julie is a very creative person who has written several books for youth in the area of spiritual growth. Julie was ordained in 1999 at the Tavistock Mennonite Church. Julie is married to Mike White, and they are expecting their first child. From 2002, Julie has been serving as a co-pastor at Wellesley Mennonite Church.

The image of ministry which has emerged for me over the past eight years is that of midwife. As a pastor, I've come to think of myself as a "spiritual midwife." Perhaps one of the most attractive aspects of this metaphor is its strongly feminine associations. A midwife's main role is to attend to a (physical) birthing. In a similar fashion, a pastor is called to attend to the spiritual birthings that occur as God works in and among the members of a church family. The process of birthing is beyond the midwife/pastor: it is God who initiates the process and determines the outcome of that process. My role as a pastor is to help facilitate new life and spiritual possibilities in others of all ages and both genders.

I love this image of helping to "birth" new life in others. As a pastor, one of my goals is to empower others; to facilitate the calling out and lifting up of others' ministry gifts and abilities for the good of the Body of Christ: the Church. 1 Peter 4:10 reminds me, "Each one should use the gift they have received to *serve others*, faithfully administering God's grace in its various forms." In the first church I pastored, I found much delight in creating and writing skits and dramatic readings for junior youth and youth to perform during worship services.

I felt like a midwife as I helped the youth practice a drama and get a feel for how it might become part of the service and the flow of worship. It was exciting to shoulder-tap and discern along with them, deciding whose dramatic gifts we could encourage and invite. On Sunday morning I experienced the joy of watching them engage in drama ministry. I simply facilitated the birthing of their talents as I called forth that which God had already created in them. I attended their spiritual birthings, watched and aided in the calling forth and enabling of the gifts God had given them. As well, I enjoyed coaching a youth/adult through the process of Worship Leading. It was a joy to empower others to lead worship. Some of these people whom I encouraged went on to study ministry at Canadian Mennonite Bible College.

A midwife's formal involvement with a mother eventually ceases. A midwife covenants with a mother/couple to be present with them for a time: to walk with them through a pregnancy and to attend to the birthing.

The midwife is not a central figure forever. She is only *one* of the persons who will figure in a child's life. Eventually, the midwife leaves the mother/baby and moves on to attend another birthing process. As a midwife-pastor, I was called by God to attend the spiritual birthings at Tavistock Mennonite Church for more than six years, after which time I felt God nudging me to move on. In January 2002 I began ministry at Wellesley Mennonite Church as one of their co-pastors. The fact that there is a temporal aspect to being a midwife is a powerful reminder that, as a pastor, I am not indispensable or immortal and will not be around in any given congregation forever.

While I am present in a church family, I must be one hundred per cent present for them and with them. But eventually God will call me to move on again. It helps to view myself as only *one* of the many persons God will call to pastor any given congregation in its lifetime. I will make certain contributions to the life and faith of a congregation, and subsequent pastors will make other contributions. The pastor is set apart in a special way that does not devalue the contributions of other church members/participants. Ordination is an acknowledgment that the pastor has a central role to play in the spiritual birthings of a congregation. His or her gifts are no more important than those of other participants but are significant in a unique manner.

My experience of Ordination was quite moving. When I began as Associate Pastor at Tavistock Mennonite Church (TMC), I was not licensed because that was not the current trend in MCEC. Five years into my term, things had changed at the Conference level and pastors were being licensed at their Installation services. When the TMC Leadership Team met to discern whether I should be licensed at that point in time, we all agreed that Ordination was more appropriate. They sensed that

God was indeed calling me to pastoral ministry. They saw evidence in my work among them that I had accepted this calling.

For my part, I had done intensive Supervised Experiences in Ministry, work with a Spiritual Director and an Integration Seminar in order to discern God's call in my life. I too felt ready to acknowledge and celebrate my pastoral calling. For me, ordination was simply that—an acknowledgment and celebration of a lifelong call to ministry. I see it as a dedication of my life to helping others experience God's presence, hear God's voice, and discover, practice and use the gifts God has given them! My ordination is one of the blessings I received from the Tavistock Mennonite Church.

It has been a joy to watch as persons of all ages make faith commitments or experience "holy moments" as they encounter the movings and groovings of God's spirit in their lives. There is nothing more precious than when a young person says, "I felt/saw God today!" I thoroughly enjoy preaching and the challenge of making the Scriptures come alive in a way that speaks to people today. I like to think of the Bible as God's holy storybook…those stories are jam-packed with gems of truth, humour, zany life experiences and tales of God's track record. To share their power with others is my passion! One of the greatest joys and challenges for me is helping to facilitate intergenerational worship experiences which engage folks of all ages!

In my experience it has been a challenge to figure out how to work in positive and healthy ways with a male colleague—to work in ways that balance power and leadership. It took me a long time to feel okay about my style of ministry as a female—and to realize how I pastored would be radically different from a male colleague just by virtue of my gender and that that style was A-OK! I feel blessed in my present team setting where we are doing some really proactive things to ensure we keep on this track! It discourages me when I hear rumblings of the "anti-women-in-leadership" debate. In this day and age, I wish we could just get over that whole issue!

My most significant contribution to ministry I would have to say, is my writing. I have written a Fastlane Bible Study for Junior Youth on the topic of friendship Another book being published is called, *Tent of Meeting: A 20-Day Spiritual Adventure with God.* It appropriates Spiritual Disciplines for youth and junior youth. My third book, a work in progress, is a compilation of my skits, readers theatres and dramas called *Joyful Noize.* My passion for writing grows from my desire to create interesting and engaging resources which help youth and people of all ages to encounter God in a meaningful way! I stumbled onto this gift when I began writing worship resources and preaching sermons. For me, paying attention to God is central to my ministry. The regular practice of Spiritual Disciplines is the fuel which powers my ministry.

As most part-time pastors know, it is often a challenge to keep part-time to part-time and not end up with oodles of overtime. I love my job as a pastor and am very passionate about it. Therefore I sometimes struggle to maintain healthy boundaries around my personal time with family, friends and self. My hope as I anticipate the birth of our child is that, although my loyalties will become a bit more divided, I will be able to creatively figure out how to continue in pastoral ministry in ways that are life-giving and adventurous, rather than draining and all-consuming. I am in the very fortunate position of having a husband whose career allows him to share childcare with me during the work week. Therefore, when I'm at work I will have peace of mind knowing that Mike is at home doing the parenting thing, and this perhaps is what makes it easiest for me to consider continuing on in ministry. I'm thrilled that our child will have opportunity to bond with both of his/her parents, and in a way that allows both of them to continue pursuing their own callings!

I feel blessed to be part of a wonderfully caring church family. Thus far in my ministry at Wellesley Mennonite there have been many persons who have cautioned me to guard my time, to be careful to take adequate time off, and to make time with Mike, my friends and family a priority. Often those in roles of support in my church will affirm me for the job I'm doing, but also wisely remind me to not take on too much. As I become a mother, I hope my church family will continue to nudge me in these healthy directions and that they will be flexible with my potentially hectic schedule after the arrival of baby Ellison White.

My prayer is that Wellesley Mennonite Church and I can be open and honest about this whole journey: I am their first female pastor and therefore the first pastor to take a maternity leave so this is "new" territory for all of us. God majors in "making things new," so for now I'm content to leave it in God's hands.

Anita Schroeder Kipfer

"My Prayer is that women and men might continue working together as equal partners in ministry, offering mutual love, respect and reciprocity as we help each other and our congregations to vision new ways of being the church in the world."
—A. S. K.

In 2003, Anita is the youngest woman pastor serving in a Mennonoite congregation in Ontario. She is a member of a team of two or three pastors at Stirling Avenue Mennonite Church in Kitchener. She and her husband Bryan are expecting their first child. From her writing, it's obvious that Anita enjoys poetry, and I share that love too. Anita writes about her struggle in accepting her call to pastoral ministry, and also her joy and satisfaction in following that call.

For everyone
The swimmer's moment at the whirlpool comes,
But many at that moment will not say
"This is the whirlpool, then."
By their refusal they are saved
From the black pit, and also from contesting

The deadly rapids, and emerging in
The mysterious, and more ample, further waters
. . .
Of those who dare the knowledge
Many are whirled into the ominous centre
That, gaping vertical, seals up
For them an eternal boon of privacy,
So that we turn away from their defeat
With a despair, not for their deaths, but for
Ourselves, who cannot penetrate their secret
Nor even guess at the anonymous breadth
Where one or two have won:
(The silver reaches of the estuary).

From "The Swimmer's Moment" by Margaret Avison. From Gary Geddes ed. *15 Canadian Poets X2*. Toronto: Oxford University Press,1988, p. 180.

I first came across this poem in a Canadian Literature class during my undergraduate studies at the University of Waterloo. I find myself returning to it again and again. It speaks of a time in each person's life when they knowingly or unknowingly must face the whirlpool. It is about leaving behind the known and familiar to venture into the mysterious unknown. This reflection is about my swimmer's moment.

Presently I am in my fourth year of ministry as a pastor at Stirling Avenue Mennonite Church where I was licensed in September, 1998. I am in ministry because I love God and the people of God, and because I love the Church. I believe the Spirit is continually transforming the world and that the Church can be a channel of God's justice and peace despite its flaws. On May 26, 2002, I was ordained in the Mennonite Church Eastern Canada. It was a wonderful day of celebration and blessing, a time of gratitude for God's faithfulness and leading in my life and ministry.

Through Bible college, seminary studies and ministry internships I discerned a call to pastoral ministry, yet my decision to be a pastor did not come easily. I had many questions about what this call would look like. I was especially apprehensive about how people would respond to a woman in leadership. I didn't want to be treated differently from my male colleagues, or be confronted continuously with the issue of whether or not women belonged in leadership positions. I simply wanted to be a pastor.

Some of this struggle stemmed from my own denomination's stance on women in ministry. Growing up in the Mennonite Brethren Church I was always surrounded by loving, devoted Christians who nurtured my spiritual gifts with their words of affirmation and encouragement, and who upheld me steadfastly in prayer. I was even invited to preach during the summer months. However, when I went to the pulpit to preach my first sermon, one gentleman stood up and walked out. I learned that another person had stayed home, knowing a woman would be in the pulpit that morning. On another occasion a man shook my hand warmly and spoke about how meaningful my sermon had been while he assured me that this did not change his perspective on women in ministry.

Many others from my home church were very supportive of my being a pastor and have continued to affirm me. I experienced a deep sense of peace during my ordination service when my former pastor blessed me with personal words of affirmation along with a blessing from my home congregation. I praise God for this healing, reconciling love. Underlying my call to ministry is a commitment to work at mutuality and gender equity in the church, and to continue building bridges of healing and reconciliation.

I have been inspired and greatly sustained through the stories and voices of other people, especially women who have faced similar obstacles in ministry and who continue surmounting them with grace, conviction, and courage. This affirms my own experience and the significance of my role in helping to envision models for creative ministry in a perpetually changing church. My prayer is two-fold: that male leaders in today's churches who condone women in leadership might assume more responsibility for implementing necessary changes in structure and practice to ensure gender equity; and secondly, that women and men might continue working together as equal partners in ministry, offering mutual love, respect and reciprocity as we help each other and our congregations to envision new ways of being the church in the world.

A helpful image of ministry for me has been that of the labyrinth; a sacred circle with a single path that leads to its center. Walking the path lends itself to prayer and meditation, essential for both my personal life and vocation. The labyrinth symbolizes life as a journey, both inward and outward. As a circle it is a universal symbol of unity and wholeness, inviting us to walk with God who encircles us and knows us through and through (Psalm 139). One can walk the labyrinth alone or in the company of others. All that is required is faithfulness to the path. The circle of the labyrinth brings to mind another wonderful image of ministry; that of a round table symbolizing warmth, openness and hospitality. Everyone in their diversity is welcome and all are treated with equal regard.

Mothering has always been something that I've anticipated and greatly looked forward to in my life. I am very excited about this part of my life's journey and am interested to see how it will all work out. I'm grateful for God's call in my life to ministry and the ways in which I've experienced a sense of affirmation and fulfillment with this calling. I love being a pastor despite all the challenges ministry brings, and I think I will also love being a mom amidst all the challenges of parenting. I wonder how pastoring and mothering will fit together in my life.

After learning about my pregnancy one member of my congregation approached me with great concern in her voice and said, "This doesn't mean you're leaving us does it?" "Well . . . I don't think so," I replied with some uncertainty. I really didn't know just how to respond. After I shared this with my husband, his comment was, "Just say: 'We're not really sure what's ahead as we've never done this before.'" That was helpful feedback, as at this point I simply don't know how having a child will affect my call to ministry. I know that so much in my life will change with the arrival of a baby. Most importantly I want to be open to God's leading for me personally, for our family and for Stirling, whether that means continuing in part-time ministry or being at home full-time. As I look ahead, both seem like realistic possibilities.

While I am the first female pastor in Stirling's history to have a baby and take a maternity leave, the congregation has been very encouraging, caring and supportive. At different times throughout my ministry at Stirling I have been cautioned to try and stay within appropriate boundaries of work and personal time. I feel I have a very open and honest relationship with the congregation and I hope that can continue. Being part of a pastoral team provides flexibility and additional support.

My swimmer's moment came when I said "Yes" to God's call to be a pastor. I'm grateful for my place in the Church and for those who have helped make it possible for women like me to be in leadership. My journey in the whirlpool is accompanied at times by great fear and uncertainty, at other times with deep gratitude and joy for the sacredness of ministry. Sometimes I question this commitment, this saying "yes" to God. The path seems so daunting and the cost too great, and I wonder with trepidation if I made the right choice. Then I see in the water my own image reflected back and God's hands supporting me, and I remember the part in the poem about courage and the silver reaches of the estuary. And I jump in again.

Hendrike Isert Bender

"I am still in the process of searching for adequate ways to maintain my calling and passion for ministry as well as my calling and passion for motherhood."
—H. I. B.

Hendrike and Matthew Isert Bender are serving the Nith Valley Mennonite Church near New Hamburg, and they are are my pastors. They have two young children—Benedikt and Tomas. Hendrike has been on a year's maternity leave since their second child was born in the spring of 2002. They have shared pastoral duties since being installed and licensed in June of 2001. In 2002-3 Matthew has assumed full-time pastoral responsibilies, but when Hendrike finishes her leave, she will again work half-time at the church.

Hendrike is an enthusiastic pastor who is interested in people of all ages. She enjoys youth and children and is involved in planning Christian Education at Nith Valley. She also preaches regularly and helps to plan for creative worship experiences. She writes about her experience in ministry and mothering with her usual candor and useful insights.

Being at the beginning of pastoral ministry as well as raising a young family, challenges are slowly emerging; and I am still in the process of searching for adequate ways to maintain my calling and passion for ministry as well as my calling and passion for motherhood. Co-pastoring with my husband is one way I can see these two demanding callings co-existing together and remain passionate and energetic for both. One reason I considered co-ministry instead of pursuing a career in social work was that I dreaded spending most of my evenings and weekends by myself raising children. It was a perception I had of many pastors' spouses in the past. We began ministry without a young family, which gave me time to realize that ministry can be all-consuming if one lets it be, and that one needs to negotiate limits and boundaries with the congregation in order to pastor effectively and to prevent early burnout.

When my husband Matthew and I re-entered ministry after a three-year absence from it, we had just started our family. We felt it was important to be open with the congregation as we were trying to find meaningful ways to nurture the faith of our children, and also walk alongside this congregation. The church has been very affirming of raising a young family and has been extremely supportive in many aspects. This does not mean that we are not facing any challenges.

Sunday morning is one of the most difficult times. It is impossible to be attentive to a conversation when one child is running down the aisle making a beeline for the microphone as people are gathering their thoughts for worship, and the other child is getting restless because naptime is fast approaching. As a couple, we have agreed that the person who is preaching is focussed on the needs of congregational members, and the other is focussed on the needs of our children. This might seem easy in theory, but much harder in practice.

Another challenge we have faced raising a young family and being in co-ministry is situations when we feel that it would be beneficial for both of us to be part of certain events. It is easy to take our infant along; our toddler is another story. As the children get older, it takes more time to deliberate which events are actually important for both of us to attend, and which events allow for children to be present. It is an issue we will continue to struggle with.

Less than a year into our ministry at our new congregation, I went on maternity leave. Being co-pastors made this transition easier for us and the congregation. My husband became the full-time pastor while I was on maternity leave. Some members might see me just as an ordinary church member while others will continue to see me as their pastor. As my maternity leave comes to an end, I feel we as co-pastors as well as the congregation were able to adjust well and appropriately to the transition. At times, however, I did struggle with my identity not knowing whether people talked to me because I was their pastor, or because I was a church member that they just felt like talking to. Maybe I need more maternity leaves to figure this out!

Maternity leaves are a new phenomenon for many churches, and it seems we are just beginning to try to figure out what to do when our female pastors are absent for one year. Barb Smith Morrison, who has had two maternity leaves, expressed the struggles and challenges for her and her congregation when she goes on leave. Transitions are difficult for congregations—especially those who already have multiple staff in which transitions can occur more often. Reflecting with other women on this issue, the question was raised as to why churches seem insecure on how to deal with those transitions. If congregations could be given some guidance on how transitions—especially those caused through maternity leaves—could be made smoother, fewer women might feel that "mother guilt" about going on another maternity leave.

For women in ministry, as with many working women, "mother guilt" seems to be a common thread. It becomes especially pronounced when the children are sick or have specific needs that require attention. The compelling feeling of wanting to be with them, and yet wanting and needing to be with church members and programs, can tear our hearts apart. It seems that many of us have not been quite able to figure out why our spouses are able to leave and stay focussed on their work while we, expecially when our children are needy, leave them, but find it much more difficult to concentrate on the tasks at hand. At the same time, ministry is one of the professions that allow for a flexible schedule at least some of the time, which allows us to attend to the needs of our children.

The calling to ministry and the calling to motherhood give us wonderful opportunities to walk alongside incredible human beings who enrich our lives, and who can drain us at the same time. I am looking forward to the continued challenges to live with both these wonderful callings.

Combining Demanding Roles

A continuing challenge for women pastors today and in the future is how to respond to one's calling as one cares for young children. A major change in society is that we have much smaller families. My mother had nine pregnancies over a period of twenty years. Raising eight children occupied most of her adult years—even though the older children helped with the younger ones. As a second youngest child, I felt that I had three mothers! Today situations vary a great deal. Some women have help and support from their own extended families. Maternity leaves are widely accepted by churches, and are very helpful to young pastors' families, but still there are no easy ways to plan for continuing ministry.

This challenge faces both the young women pastors and the congregations they serve. Women in pastoral ministry are a varied group with some having more energy than others, some with a natural bent toward homemaking, and others who most enjoy the preparing of sermons and other pastoral tasks. Both ministry and mothering can be very demanding of time and energy at unexpected times. Caring for those who are sick or in crisis at home or in the church can be exhausting.

Women may be reluctant to name these heavy demands because in the past the simple response—especially from other women—has been that perhaps it has not been part of God's plan for women to be pastors. However, I find that too simplistic in light of the way many young women are working in other demanding vocations, and also in view of my own understanding that God is calling women to ministry in a new way at this time in the life of the church. I also believe that some women have a calling to home-making and parenting, and that they could use and share those gifts with the church. While many young couples today struggle with issues relating to two careers, a unique and stressful aspect for pastoral couples is that their dilemma is "on stage" in full view of a congregation of many people with many opinions.

Supportive congregations could find some creative ways to respond to young women pastors as they assess their resources for child-care. In several congregations, I know that young youth sponsors were helped with childcare so that they could continue to serve. Perhaps we could help young pastoral couples with their childcare responsibilities. A break from ministry for five or six years may be a good solution. Some negotiation with the Church offices of MCEC, or even notations on resumes, might help to provide continuity in ministry for women pastors with small children. The one-year maternity leave, which is now funded, could provide a good opportunity for a student or a pastor who might want to work for a year only. Male pastors with young children also have a dilemma, but I think the challenge for women is greater, at least at this point. The young women pastors who have written about their struggles with their two callings have opened up an area which is a current challenge for Mennonite churches in Ontario at a time when many pastors are needed.

Pastors and Mothers

Jan Steckley
Assistant Pastor, Steinmann Mennonite Church 1987–89; Assoc. Pastor, Breslau Mennonite Church 1989–1998; Ordained June,1994; Pastor, Hillcrest Mennonite Church, New Hamburg 1998 – Present; MTS Conrad Grebel College, University of Waterloo, 1987 to present.

Ann Weber Becker
Pastor, First Mennonite Church, Kitchener 1987-95; Ordained in 1990; Writer of Mennonite Confession of Faith youth material, *Faith for the Journey*. Executive producer of "Songs to Live By" recordings. M.Div. AMBS 1987. B. Ed. University of Western Ontario 2002.

Julie Ellison White
Assoc. Pastor, Tavistock Mennonite Church 1994 – 2000; Ordained November 14, I999; Interim at Listowel Mennonite Church June - August, 2000; Co-Pastor, Wellesley Mennonite Church 2001 to Present; B.Th CMBC MTS studies CGUC 1996 to present.

Anita Schroeder Kipfer
Pastoral Intern, Pleasant Oaks Mennonite Church, Middlebury, Indiana 1996 – 97; Stirling Ave. Mennonite Church - 1998 – Present; Ordained - May 26, 2002; Chaplain, Parkwood Mennonite Home 1998 – 2001; M. Div. AMBS 1998.

Hendrike Isert Bender
Assistant Pastor, St. Catharines United Mennonite Church 1995-98; Co-pastor, Nith Valley Mennonite Church, New Hamburg, 2001 to present; Licensed June, 2001; B.Th CMU 1994 M.S.W. WLU 2000.

Vision ForThe Future

In my first letter to women pastors in Ontario Mennonites churches, I had asked them what their vision would be for the church and for women pastors in the church of the future. Their responses to these questions were very thoughtful and stimulating, and I want to quote them directly.

My vision for women pastors in the Mennonite Church is that their gifts be identified, affirmed, and increasingly used, so that all congregations have an opportunity to experience balanced female/male ministry. They can then grow through the complementarity of male and female personalities and pastoral styles.

—Mary Burkholder

My hope for women pastors is that the day will soon be here when placement and search committees no longer have a blank for gender on their forms. It would indicate that gender is inconsequential. My vision goes on to see women function in ministry using all of their gifts of womanhood, and not needing to function as a male to be accepted. As these women bring their gifts of femininity, and as they serve alongside of men, a wholeness of life and vision is demonstrated and celebrated as together they share the Good News.

—Doris Weber

My vision for women pastors is that they have the opportunity to respond to God's call to ministry, to prepare themselves for ministry, and to use their gifts as God leads. My vision is that at every level the church will be open to call and to use those women whom God calls. My vision is that all women who experience God's call will demonstrate Christian maturity in their lives and attitudes and ministry. My vision is that all children and youth in our churches will have positive role models of female and male pastoral leadership, and that girls as well as boys will be encouraged to listen for God's call.
—Helen Reusser

My prayer is that our daughters and granddaughters, as well as our sons and grandsons, will have the freedom to receive and respond to God's call to pastoral ministry, without worrying whether it will be their gender that determines whether or not the church will receive them as well.
—Doreen Neufeld

Some of my dreams for female ministers are: that female ministers within ten years of retirement may be able to retire in peace!; that more females may have opportunity to lead a staff team; and that female ministers may be able to navigate their way through the difficult decisions of their childbearing and child-raising years. Finally, my vision is that pastoral ministry may be shaped in such a way that both men and women can see a place for themselves in it.
—Sue Steiner

My vision for women pastors in the Mennonite Church is that women be accepted for the gifts God has given them. Women are still in the minority, although in MCEC women have received more encouragement than in other areas in Canada.
—Catherine Hunsberger

Other hopeful and significant comments about the future and about their vision for it have been scattered throughout the stories of the twenty-four women who responded in this project. My own vision is that in the future women will be called according to their gifts as they are needed in particular congregations. Some will choose to work on mixed-gender teams, others will be the sole pastors in congregations, a few will hold positions of responsibility in the office of the Mennonite Church of Eastern Canada or of Mennonite Church Canada, and some will work in special ministry such as chaplaincy, youth ministry or interim pastorates. I hope that churches will not only call, but also affirm and support women in their various ministries.

I hope that will also happen for the men who minister in the Mennonite Church of Eastern Canada. And I believe that men and women working together in the church bring a combination of gifts that will add creativity and vitality to the Mennonite Churches in Ontario and elsewhere. Human nature being what it is, and knowing my own humanity as I do, I have never been optimistic enough to say that if women were completely in charge things would be so much better. I think the church might be somewhat different, but my best scenario for the future lies in women and men working together in ministry. I do think that women as a group offer somewhat different abilities, and that when we are faithful to how God has created and gifted us we will act and speak in unique and new ways. Over time it will affect the language of worship, and I look forward to the day when some of the male pronouns will sound quaint and old-fashioned. Women do need to speak with integrity as well as authority.

The early women pastors who were pioneers, and none of us who were the first women to serve in pastoral leadership in a congregations had role models for ministry. While that has changed somewhat, the same vacuum exists in some places.

Maybe each generation needs some new models for ministry. Anne Campion, who works with youth across Canada, says, "Young people today continue to need models for women pastors. Women's ministry grows out of relationship and connectedness. I hope that as women pastors we would see God's call to us as a gift to the Church and not about proving ourselves."

Muriel Bechtel, our current Minister of Pastoral Services, writes with hope for the future: I look forward to the day when I won't have to ask search committees and congregations whether they are "ready" or "willing" to have a female pastor; when the combination of gifts, personality, leadership style and experience will be more important than gender in the selection of a pastor; when women will not have to try twice as hard to prove themselves and be twice as good to get pastoral positions comparable to those available to male candidates; when there will be equal numbers of women and men in ministry and in lead pastor positions; when young women will be "tapped on the shoulder" and encouraged to consider pastoral ministry as often as young men are; when both men and women will be freed by their congregations to take parental leaves or work part-time in ministry for a while in order to give their young families the time and attention they need.

I asked two of our younger women pastors who are pregnant with a first child what their hopes are for the future in relation to their pastoral calling. Julie Ellison White wrote: "As a woman who is already juggling 'the balls' of part-time pastoring, a writing career, many volunteer commitments, and family relationships, I'm probably most anxious about taking on another 'ball' to juggle! While I am very excited and can't wait to welcome our first child, I worry about what sort of shifts and adjustments will have to happen in order to continue working outside the home." *Anita Schroeder Kipfer commented:* "My hope as we anticipate the birth of our child is that I will be able to discern God's leading in my life so as to know both where and how God is calling me as I reflect on my roles as mom and pastor. I am looking forward to what the months ahead hold, both for me personally and for Stirling, as we trust God's leading and find our way together."

These hopes and fears have been shared openly and honestly by these young women on the brink of motherhood. I recall Ingrid Loepp Thiessen, who resigned from pastoral work after her third child was born, saying that she had two passions in life—mothering and pastoring. It was a tough decision to give up one of those even for a few years. Other younger women pastors have made difficult choices for the sake of their families. Our vision for the future should include ways of honouring their callings and their gifts for pastoral ministry during the child-bearing years so that they will be able to continue in ministry or return to it as God leads them and as they discern that leading together with their spouses and churches.

Most of the women who responded made comments about the future of the church. I will repeat a few more of them.

"What is my vision? I wonder how to pass on the torch for Urban Ministry where there is much room and need for women pastors." —Doris Kipfer

I believe that if the Christian Church is to survive and thrive in the new, ever-changing world, it must shift from a model of the competitive, efficiently-run business to the model of a centre for belonging and networking. To make this shift, women need to bring their feminine perspectives to the table: the gifts of creativity, compassion and nurturing relationships. It is not enough for us to break into the realm of male

leadership and learn to lead the way men do; the Church needs us to lead the way our own hearts, and the heart of God, call us to lead.
—Renate Klaassen

In the future church, I hope that gender (in the negative sense) becomes a non-issue—that girls and women no longer feel denigrated. I am concerned that women equally with men, receive encouragement, funding, and opportunity in relation to their sense of call and studies toward ministry. Women and girls should be included equally with men and boys in the life of the church.
—Bertha Landers

My own vision for the church has been strengthened by the responses of these twenty-four women pastors. I find hope in the variety of personalities, styles of ministry, and life experiences which they have brought to their pastoral work. By now younger women do have some models for ministry, and these models are diverse. In the end each woman or man who responds to God's call to be a pastor will have to forge her or his own pastoral identity and it will be unique. I am convinced by what God has been doing, through the gifts and commitment of women pastors in Ontario, that God will continue to call young women as well as young men to pastoral ministry.

I find hope in the fact that so many churches in Ontario have called women as pastors, and that people have been open to their ministry. By now many more churches have experienced the ministry of women as pastors. As we have ministered and as people have learned to know and trust us, we have sensed that who we are as persons created by God is more important than gender. In one of my first church settings people seemed to prefer to call me "Mary" rather than "Pastor," and I decided that if that was their choice, I preferred to be called by name rather than by any title. We minister out of who we really are.

Not the End of the Story

A number of women have commented on the meaning and significance of ordination in relation to their calling and their work in pastoral ministry. While men also have celebrated ordination, it may have had added significance for women since it has been more difficult for women to receive authority in the church. Part of that struggle may be that women minister in some different ways. Relationships are very important to women, and authority may come from the depth and power of the way a woman pastor relates to the congregation. It is hard to discern at times; and even harder to name such authority as power. A professor I once had said that he thought the basis of all authority in the Church is love. If that is true, then it is easier to discern a woman pastor's authority through relationship; but it is also true that male pastors have authority based on love and relationships. It has always seemed ironic to me that unless people accept and respond to one's ministry, it is impossible to do ministry at all. A very humbling reality which points to love and a deep acceptance as the basis and power for all pastoral ministry.

Many women pastors had earlier training and experience in nursing, social work, or teaching. They brought this useful backgroundand their giftedness for pastoring to their work in ministry. In their stories several women demonstrate that their gifts of counseling or evangelism are unique in the settings in which they minister. The discovery and development of gifts for pastoral ministry in places far from where we grew up is also a factor for women who served as missionaries abroad. These women missionaries also had an influence on a number of the early women pastors. My own experience of teaching in Kenya became part of my sense of call to ministry.

When I look back, I realize that pastoral work has been a gift to me in many ways. The built in priorities of attention to my faith and to prayer, to study and reflection on Scripture, to caring for others, to facing death with courage and hope, and learning to live with differing beliefs and convictions, have been great benefits to me. Overall and more indirectly, they have been blessings to my family too. In a time when many options and many choices compete for priority and time in our lives, my calling has often determined what choices I made and what path I walked. I also learned to appreciate the simple pleasures of family life, of small caring groups, and of daily challenges that test, but do not overwhelm me. Ministry has encouraged me to learn more about prayer as a personal resource to renew my courage and strength, and to find balance in life's ups and downs.

My farewell sermon at Hillcrest also reflects my movement into retirement, and I am repeating from it what I believe may relate to other congregations as well:

As I say goodbye at Hillcrest, there certainly are things that I am thankful for, and I expect that in the future some other things will come to mind. And then, like Paul does in Philippians, I will thank God for you. I am grateful for the opportunity of serving here in this place for the past six years. It has been a rich experience of ministry for me. I recall baptismal services and parent-child dedications, communion and footwashing services, and funerals and weddings in this sanctuary. I recall a summer Sunday when I had told the story of the woman who met Jesus at the well, and when we invited people to come to drink water as a symbol of God's grace, everyone came! A host of memories come as I recall my ministry (often together with Maurice) in this place.

I am also thankful for what I have learned about community at Hillcrest. You are respectful of the feelings people have, and you listen to different views expressed by individuals as you process decisions. You work to include new persons in the church family. Hillcrest is not a perfect community, but a real and vital one. This congregation is centered around Jesus Christ, and I am thankful that my contributions to building up the church have been taken seriously. I have been impressed by the gift discernment you do, and by how you are able to make changes.

I am also thankful for the special privilege ministry has given me in this church family. You welcomed me into your homes and into your lives at very important and at some difficult times. When you have been sick or in pain or grief, you have shared that experience with me. I have enjoyed visiting with you, and sharing in your happy or sad times in life. We are thankful too for both of the cluster groups George and I have belonged to, and for other small groups that met for book study or for anointings and for Winter Wednesday nights. To quote Philippians again "It is only natural that I should feel like this about you all—you are very dear to me."

Philippians also has some direction for the focus of my prayers for this congregation now and in the future. I pray that your love will increase. Love for God and for each other. Paul prays that it will increase in knowledge and wise insight. We have experienced some challenges in loving each other—some had to do with abuse within families, for *example, and so forced us to face things we might rather avoid. We have been and will be challenged to learn more about loving persons with different sexual orientations. My prayer is that you will grow in your love and acceptance of many persons who struggle in various ways. We will all need to grow in knowledge and wisdom in order to love wisely and well.*

I pray that you will be discerning as you set your priorities in life. Sometimes I sense that family has become the highest priority. We must remember that Jesus said that his disciples were his family—as high a priority as his mother and his brothers and sisters. Be as loyal to your church family as you are to your biological family! Be sincere and truthful about your priorities. You can not neglect your children or spouse in favour of the church; but as appropriate, you also should not neglect the church family either. You need the support and teaching of the church in order to recognize the highest and best in your life. I pray that God's Spirit will guide you when you think about what is important in life.

I pray that your lives will be full of true goodness. What does that mean for you? I do not know the specifics, and you do not know what that may mean in the future. I pray that you will grow more and more into the persons that God created you to be with the help of the teachings of Jesus and through the direction and power of God's Spirit.I pray that you will continue to serve others in practical ways that demonstrate the grace of our Lord Jesus Christ.

I pray that you will live to the praise and glory of God. At times when I think of you—especially if I am concerned about you for some reason—I will pray as I often have when I have been with you—that God will surround you with love and care in a special way. As you and I know, it is not always easy to love each other or others in the community or even in our families. But I pray that you will help each other in that. Leaving is not easy either as we know just now. We will miss your friendship and support. So we invite you to pray for us too when you remember us.

To again express my thanks to you, God's people at Hillcrest, I want to close with part of this poem which expresses how I feel about serving God in this church:

> *It is good to have stood long enough in life to have found cour-
> age and gratitude in my heart*
> *To sing for others and to God the deepest song of my heart.*
> *The song is not made by me, but is given through me.*
> *I have tried to be faithful to the great Music through which it is
> given.*
> *Gratitude is my deepest song of heart.*
> *And I sing my song of heart immeasurably not alone.*
> *From "In Praise of Gratitude" by Robert Raynolds. Harper &
> Brothers, 1961, p. 185.*

Pastoral work must be quite a healthy profession. Among the twenty-four women pastors quoted in this book, almost all are in good health, and there have been no deaths. Of course, it is a stressful and chaotic life at times, but there have been resources of faith and hope, of caring, supportive church communities, and occasions of joy and celebration. In Ontario, churches have been fair in the salaries which they paid to women pastors. While ordination was an empowerment for most women pastors, other things also kept us going. The encouragement of a spouse was very important for some. For most of us, experiences in ministry that validated our sense of call, and our satisfaction in the work itself were significant. It is clear from responses that these women pastors have found their ministry assignments to be both a joy and a challenge. It is also evident that God has blessed and guided these pastors and the congregations where they worked.

Articulateness, capability, charm, insight and tact are qualities that enhance our ministry, and these twenty-four women do possess these characteristics in varying combinations and degrees. However, I deeply believe that unless such qualities are firmly grounded in our faith in God, the Giver of such gifts, and in our calling to pastoral ministry, they can become self-serving and superficial. The challenge for us as women leaders is to recognize that our greatest efforts are part of God's work, and that what is fruitful and lasting in the churches where we have served is ultimately the amazing work of God's Spirit. As I have collected this material and written this book, I have prayed, "The work of our hands and of our hearts, establish Thou it, O God."

If I have been "preachy" at times in this book, I hope you will understand that it is an occupational hazard! I noticed that tendency in the responses from some other women pastors too. We trust that you will forgive such bits of sermonizing as we have at times spoken strongly. The perspective and views expressed are uniquely my own; and I will acknowledge that all of the biases do belong to me. This book reflects my experience, reflections, and wisdom along with the experience and wisdom of other women pastors. In a way all of the women who responded could be called pioneers. I hope this book is a worthy tribute to their courage, strength, and faith.

Abbreviations

AMBS	Associated Mennonite Biblical Seminaries, Elkhart, IN
CAPPE	Canadian Association of Practice and Pastoral Education
CGC	Conrad Grebel College, Waterloo
CGUC	Conrad Grebel University College since 2002
CMBC	Canadian Mennonite Bible College, Winnipeg
CMU	Canadian Mennonite University, Winnipeg
D. Min.	Doctor of Ministry
GC	General Conference (Mennonite Church)
MCC	Mennonite Central Committee or Mennonite Church Canada
MCEC	Mennonite Conference of Eastern Canada
	Since 2001 Mennonite Church Eastern Canada
MCOQ	Mennonite Conference of Ontario and Quebec
M. Div.	Master of Divinity
M. T. S.	Master of Theological Studies
TST	Toronto School of Theology
UM	United Mennonite
UW	University of Waterloo
WLS	Waterloo Lutheran Seminary
WMSC	Women's Mission and Service Commission
WOM	Western Ontario Mennonite (Conference)

Other Women Who Have Served In Chaplaincy and In Ministry In Ontario Mennonite Churches (1973-2003)

Susan Allison-Jones

Conference Youth Minister 1988-99; Ordained September 15, 1996; Associate Pastor, Breslau Mennonite Church 1998-2003; B.R.S. Nazarene College, Winnipeg 1982 M.T.S. Candidate, CGUC 2003.

Wanda Roth Amstutz

Grace Mennonite Church, St. Catharines, 2000 to present; Ordained, Scottdale Mennonite Church, Pa. November, 1998; M.Div. AMBS 1996.

Else Barg

Chaplain Ottawa Civic Hospital 1989-95; Ordained, November 13, 1983 at Charleswood Mennonite Church, Winnipeg.

Gail Berg-Roth

Youth Pastor, Niagara United Mennonite Church, 1993-98; Steinmann Mennonite Church 1998-2000; Licensed September 20, 1998.

Ilene Bergen

MCEC Minister of Christian Education, 1994 to present; Licensed March 26, 2000.

Kara Carter

Youth Minister, Poole Mennonite Church 2002 to present; Licensed March 16, 2003.

Ruth Ann Carter
Youth Minister, Listowel Mennonite Church, 2000 to present.
Katie Derksen
Youth and Young Adult Minister, Ottawa Mennonite Church, 2000 to present, Licensed September 24, 2000.
Tanya Dyck Steinmann
Youth Minister, First Mennonite Church, Kitchener 1996- 2001; Licensed Sept. 21, 1999.
Eleanor Epp-Stobbe
Co-pastor Hamilton Mennonite Church 1985-91; Ordained in 1988.
Elsie Epp
Pastor Wildwood Mennonite Church, Saskatoon, Sask., 1978-90; Ordained 1980; Conference Minister in Conference of Mennonites of Saskatchewan,1990-96; Pastor, East Zorra Mennonite Church, Tavistock, 1996 to Present.
Sue Fallon
Markham Area Youth Minister, 1996 to present; Licensed Jan. 9, 2000.
Carrie Harder
Pastoral Care Worker, Stirling Ave. Mennonite Church 1988-1997; Licensed November 24, 1996.
Anna Hemmendinger
Pastor, Olive Branch Mennonite Church, Waterloo, 1992-97;
Licensed April 4, 1993, St. Jacobs Mennonite Church, St. Jacobs 1997-99; M.T.S. WLS 2001.
Jean Hung
Assistant Pastor, Markham Chinese Mennonite Church 1994-96.

Wendy Janzen
Youth Pastor Oak St. Mennonite Church, Leamington 1998 -2000; Licensed July 4, 1999; Associate Pastor, St. Jacobs Mennonite Church 2002-present; M.Div. 2002.

Phyllis Kramer
Interim Pastor, Steinmann Mennonite Church, Baden, 2001-present; Licensed May 13, 2001.

Jan Kraus
Chaplain, St. Michael's Hospital, Toronto, 1980 to present; Ordained, Oct. 18, 1987; Executive Director CAPPE; Co-ordinating Chaplain Huronia Regional Centre, 2002 to present; M.Div. AMBS 1983; Teaching supervisor CAPPE.

Ruth Anne Laverty
Pastor Elmira Mennonite Church, 1991 to present; Ordained October 30, 1994; M.A. WLU 1974; M.Th. WLS 1990.

Jean Lehn-Epp
Pastor, Mississauga Mennonite Fellowship 1995-2002; Licensed September 26, 1999.

Norma Lelless
Chaplain, Sunnybrook Hospital, Toronto, 1999 to present; Licensed December 5 1999, and December 15, 2002.

Ingrid Loepp Thiessen
Pastor Steinmann Mennonite Church, Baden 1991-97; Ordained, June 5, 1994; Shantz Mennonite Church, Baden, 2002 to present; M.Div AMBS 1990.

Laura Loewen
Pastor, Mennonite Fellowship of Montreal, 1988-2000; Ordained June 12, 1994; M.Div. AMBS 1998.

Audrey Mierau-Bechtel

Pastor, Harrow Mennonite Church, 1986-88; Licensed June, 1986; Chaplain, Fairview Mennonite Home, 2000 to present; Licensed Sept. 30, 2001; M.Div AMBS 1985.

Marnie Mierau-Friesen

Youth Minister, North Leamington Mennonite Church 1994-98.

Ruth Martin

Chaplain, Coordinator of Pastoral Care Services, Greenwood Court and Nithview Home, 1999 to present; Ordained December 8, 2002.

Sherri Martin

Waterford Mennonite Church, Goshen, IN, Interim Minister of Worship, 1996; Tavistock Mennonite Church, 2001 to present; Licensed September 23, 2001; M.Div, AMBS 1997.

Barb Smith Morrison

St. Jacobs Mennonite Church, 1997 to present; Licensed, 1997; To be ordained in 2003; M.T.S. CGUC in process.

Young-Jee Na

Co-pastor, Valleyview Mennonite Church, Korean Congregation, London, 1997 to present; Licensed June 10, 2001; B.Th.Canadian Mennonite Bible College 1997.

Marianne Mellinger

Ordained, April 1, 1994, Franconia Conference, Pa.; Interim Pastor, Preston Mennonite Church, 2001 to present.

Shannon Neufeldt

Assistant Pastor, Welcome Inn 1994-97; Toronto United Mennonite Church and Danforth Mennonite, 1999 to present; Licensed Jan. 31, 1999.

Carol Penner
Chaplain, Hotel Dieu Hospital, St. Catharines, 2000-02; Ordained, April 21, 2002; Interim Pastor, Welcome Inn 2003; MCEC Minister of Peace, Justice and Social Concerns 2003.

Ingrid Derry Peters
Pastor, Kingston Mennonite Fellowship,1991-99; Ordained Feb. 13, 1999.

Janet Peters
Youth Minister, North Leamington Mennonite Church, 1998-2002; Licensed Sept. 19, 1999.

Monica Pries Klassen
Youth Minister, Waterloo-Kitchener United Mennonite Church, Waterloo 1992-98.

Betty Kennedy Puricelli
Pastor New Life Faith Community, Toronto, 1983 to present; Ordained, January 29, 1984.

Shirley Redekop
Assistant Minister, Floradale Mennonite Church, 1997-2000; Director of Christian Service Ministry for Mennonite Church Canada, February, 2002 to present; Licensed April 14, 2002.

Melita Rempel
Chaplain, Limberlost Community, London 1985-87; Ordained, May 24 1987.

Marilyn Rudy Froese
Chaplain, Fairview Mennonite Home, 1992-2000;
Ordained, June 15, 1997;   M.Div.AMBS 1991.

Anna-Lisa Salo
Pastor, Waters Mennonite Church, Lively, 1993-98; Ordained, November 12, 1995; Oak St. Mennonite Church, Leamington, 2002 to present; M.Div AMBS 2000.

Ann Shertzer
Assistant to Pastor, Niagara United Mennonite Church, Niagara-on-the-Lake, 1999 to present.

Shirley Schultz
Interim Co-pastor, Hawkesville Mennonite Church, 2001 – 2003; Licensed September 30, 2001.

Colleen Shantz
Conference Youth Minister, 1985-88; Licensed November 30, 1985.

Judy Shantz
Milverton Mennonite Fellowship; Licensed February 28, 1999; Co-Pastor, Zurich Mennonite Church, 2000-2003.

Eleanor Snyder
MCEC Minister of Christian Education, 1988-94; Commissioned for ministry in wider church, September, 1989.

Beverly Suderman-Gladwell
Vineland United Mennonite, 1986-88; Erie View Mennonite Church, Port Rowan, 1991- 96; Licensed, 1991; Chaplain, Parkwood Mennonite Home, Waterloo, 2002 to present; M. Div AMBS 1991.

Pam Tolmay
Listowel Mennonite Church, 1988-90; Ordained, 1988 Goshen, IN; M.Div AMBS 1990; Ordination recognized by United Church, 1995; Atwood United Church Pastoral Charge, 1990-98; Trinity United Church, London, 1999 to present.

Phyllis Tribby
Interim Pastor, St. Jacobs Mennonite Church 1996-97; Preston Mennonite Church 1998-99; Fairview Mennonite Home, 1995-96 and 1997-98; Licensed June 28 1999; Pastor, Arvada Mennonite Church, Col., 2000 to present.

Angela Wagler
Elder River of Life Fellowship, Kitchener, 1995-2001; Licensed November 7, 1999.

Mary Wagler
Apostolic Team Ministry, 1995-98; Living Water Mennonite Fellowship, New Hamburg; Licensed, November 24, 1996.

Donita Wiebe Neufeld
Associate Pastor, Wanner Mennonite Church and Chaplain, Fairview Mennonite Home (Summers), Cambridge, ON 1989-91; Co-pastor, First Mennonite Church, Edmonton, AB; Licensed April 21, 2002; M.Div. CMU 1998.

Kim Wideman
Youth Pastor, Poole Mennonite Church, 1996-2000; Licensed June 20, 1999.

Ruth Isaac Wiederkehr
Interim Pastor, Welcome Inn, 1997-98; Licensed January 25, 1998.

Rebecca Yoder Neufeld
First Mennonite Church, Kitchener, 1992-2000; Licensed September 15, 1996; M.Div. AMBS 1981.

Lynne Williams
Chaplain, Kensington Village and Longworth Retirement Centre, London, 1997 to present; Licensed June 28, 1998; M.T.S. CGC 1996; Further Training with CAPPE.

Connie Zehr

Associate Pastor, Warden Woods Mennonite Church, 1980-87; Licensed May 12, 1982.

Notes:

The above list includes chaplains, women pastors, and youth ministers who have served at least two years in a Mennonite church or other ministry settings in Ontario.

The number of chaplains and women pastors in Ontario Mennonite Churches who were ordained between 1978 and 2003 (including commissioned status) is around forty. A few of them were ordained outside of Ontario, although they served in Ontario for some years. Several of these women are now retired. Ordination follows a period of time of licensing in the Mennonite Church, and happens at the request of the congregation and with the agreement of the Leadership Commission.

In 2003, the number of women licensed for ministry is about twenty. Normally licensing is for two years; it can be renewed, but ends when the person leaves the position. What quite often happens is that the Leadership Commission allows for reactivating a license if the period between assignments is not too lengthy. As the list shows, a few persons have been licensed a second time. Some of the women have moved out of Ontario, and thus will be credentialed elsewhere.

About the Author

Mary Schiedel grew up near Baden, Ontario, where she now lives. She taught in her home school, S.S. 16, Wilmot, in Moose Factory in northern Ontario, in Kenya in East Africa, and at Rockway Mennonite School in Kitchener during her thirteen years as a teacher. She was in pastoral ministry for thirteen years in Mennonite churches in Cambridge, Elmira and New Hamburg.

Since Mary retired from pastoral ministry five years ago, she has written "A Journey of Faith," the history of Shantz Mennonite Church, the church she attended and joined as she grew up. In addition to writing, Mary enjoys reading, walking, and gardening. Mary and her husband George spend several months in Florida each winter.

Mary has four sons, four daughters-in-law, and ten grandchildren. She enjoys relating to them as they are now moving through their teen years and into their early twenties.

Mary is a member of Nith Valley Mennonite Church south of New Hamburg. She will be serving a four-month interim as pastor at East Zorra Mennonite Church near Tavistock in the summer and fall of 2003.